In Praise of *Matte*

Allison Fine has written the essential guide for organizational success in the social age. One of those rare books that actually achieves what it explains. For an organization, nothing matters more than *Matterness.*

— Ken Segall, Author, *Insanely Simple*

Matterness makes a compelling and uplifting case for how our world is changing to honor the value of every single one of us. Fine explores the technologies, institutions and, yes, people who are helping usher in this new age of individual human dignity. Maybe it took the digitally immaterial to finally show what it means to matter.

— Douglas Rushkoff, Author, *Present Shock: When Everything Happens Now*

Allison Fine has done it again! She lays out the concept of *Matterness* by offering best practices, stories, and examples of ways of working for organization as they ride the second wave of the social media revolution.

— Beth Kanter, Author, Beth's Blog

Matterness provides an essential framework for understanding why people and organizations matter so much to each other right now. This book is packed with great stories and important lessons, and should be mandatory reading for leaders of all organizations.

— Susan Crawford, Author, *Captive Audience*

matter•ness

fearless leadership for a social world

ALLISON H. FINE

Matterness: fearless leadership for a social world

For information about this title or to order other books and/or electronic media, contact the publisher:
Legacy Books, LLC
legacybooksllc.wordpress.com
legacybooksllc@gmail.com

ISBNs:
978-0-9905777-0-6 (hardcover)
978-0-9905777-1-3 (softcover)
978-0-9905777-2-0 (e-book)

Printed in the United States of America

Cover and Interior design: 1106 Design

Book Cover Text: Graham Van Dixhorn, Write to Your Market, Inc.

To my parents, Joan and Jerry, who taught me
to keep my eye on the ball, swing level,
and treat every person with dignity and respect.

Table of Contents

Prologue

TRAVELING THROUGH THE Milwaukee airport was turning into another desultory flying experience. The collective mood of the travelers was one of reluctant acceptance as we snaked through the long security line, shifting under the weight of carryons and mindfully holding boarding passes and IDs. Then came my turn to approach the scanners and with it the intense pressure to quickly and publicly unravel. *Shoes off! Jacket off! Take everything out of your pockets!* I pushed the grey bins through the X-ray machine and stepped gingerly through the metal detector with my hands in the air in surrender — the only gesture I could legally make — wondering, as always, why a belt buckle sets the machinery off but underwire doesn't. Safely on the other side, I grabbed my belongings, and shuffled over to a bench to put myself back together. And there I saw a big sign:

RECOMBOBULATION AREA

Oh, what a perfect word! It not only captured my immediate need to put myself back together in the airport, but it also perfectly conveyed our need to put ourselves back together individually and collectively after a long period of personal disempowerment and organizational ineffectiveness.

We are living in a moment of tremendous economic, social, and technological disruption that, by its very nature, has left many people desperately trying to find a foothold to steady themselves. One result of these disruptions, catalyzed by the spread of social media, is the shift in power from institutions to individuals — from music companies to musicians, from journalists to bloggers, from imperious, tone-deaf corporations to consumers. Individuals have more power to shape their lives than at any other time in history. Not always, not universally, but enough to restore the hope that after several centuries, the norm of institutional dominance is beginning to change.

Even with this silver lining of personal empowerment, the move from a world ordered by large institutions to a disaggregated and atomized one, with everyone seemingly on her own socially and economically, has been unsettling for most people. However, even though it can feel like a free-for-all, it isn't. Rather, it is a new way of living and working together that combines the natural strengths we have as people: Our creativity and generosity, our need to connect with other people in meaningful ways, and our desire to control our own futures, *together* with the power of organizations to gather resources, provide products and services at scale, and sustain efforts over time. This powerful intersection is "Matterness." It is the shared space that balances the needs of both people and organizations and enables both to thrive.

The emergence of social media has provided an exhilarating ride for me personally over the past ten years. It has been a decade filled with creative political campaigns, heartwarming stories of generosity and kindness that have gone viral, and entrepreneurial dreams becoming realities as a result of online platforms.

Conversely, bullies have used social media to belittle less-fortunate or less-powerful people. Con men have found a whole new terrain to hone their craft. In the name of "national security" or "commerce," powerful forces have used the easy aggregation of unprecedented amounts of personal data to destroy any pretense of privacy we may have had. Companies like Twitter and Facebook are transforming customers into commodities to satisfy their need for greater profits.

The current disruption is not our first experience with serious social upheavals. We have been here before — during the Civil War, the Industrial Revolution, the upheavals of the 1960s, and as with every time before, we are again in search of answers to important questions: Are we living up to our principles and promise? Will our children be able to live productive and prosperous lives? Can we find a middle ground between self-interest and community concern? The difference this time is that our search is powered by a powerful new technological toolset that spreads our desires, fears, and concerns wider, faster, and louder.

Our charge right now is to focus on what we do best: Being creative and generous people, and fearlessly leading organizations that solve problems and serve people well. This will ensure that the needs and interests of both people and organizations are met and that we are collectively creating a healthy, prosperous, and just society. This book is intended to help us navigate the right pathways to meet these lofty goals.

Introduction

HUMAN HANDS THAT HAVE BEEN wet for seventy-two hours resemble those of a drowned cadaver—ghostly white, wrinkled, and swollen. Paul Benedict's 63-year-old hands looked like those of a dead man, but Paul wasn't dead. He was homeless during a record rainfall in Los Angeles County in December 2010. Los Angeles County averages about fifteen inches of rainfall a year, but nearly half of that total came down in December alone. For days, the skies just kept emptying water on southern California. Paul was one of more than six hundred homeless men in Los Angeles County who had to remain outside in the rain because the homeless shelters were closed during the day.

Mark Horvath and his Twitter followers came to Paul's rescue. Mark was a case manager for a homeless shelter in Los Angeles at the time. That's his Clark Kent identity. On Twitter, he is a superhero who goes by the name "Hardly Normal" and has nearly 20,000 followers. Some of Mark's online friends are also advocates for the homeless, but most aren't. Most are kind and generous people who follow Mark to find out how to bring comfort to people.

Mark knew that the most likely places for homeless people to try to hide from torrential rain in Los Angeles were beneath highways and in culverts. That's where he went to recruit people to shelters, providing real-time Twitter updates and requests for help as he went. His Twitter followers responded with an outpouring of food, socks, clothing, and blankets. A few weeks later, one woman drove five hours to deliver a walker for a homeless, disabled woman Mark had tweeted about.

At the same time that he was tweeting about the needs of individual homeless people, Mark was also posting messages about the injustice of hundreds of homeless people forced outside during the torrential rainstorm. He posted videos of himself on his YouTube channel, *InvisiblePeopleTV,* standing outside in the pouring rain, excoriating the state government for not providing full-day shelter relief. The local news media picked up Mark's story. Finally, Governor Schwarzenegger opened the National Guard Armories to provide full-day shelter relief during the rainy season.

Fast-forward two years, and Hurricane Sandy has just devastated New York City. Mark took to Twitter again and asked his friends on the East Coast, "Can you find several generators?" Finding a generator right after Hurricane Sandy in New York City was like winning the lottery — a single hope with hopeless odds. But, within several hours, two men with three generators were driving to lower Manhattan.

Before Mark worked at a homeless shelter, he worked for a television syndication distribution company. In between these two jobs, he was homeless. He was also a drug dealer and a small-time crook, among other things. Mark worked hard to rebuild his life; he found religion, got sober, and began counseling other people. And then he was laid off again, and his economic troubles spiraled out of control again. This time, Mark found his voice and salvation by starting *InvisiblePeopleTV* and eventually landed a job at a homeless shelter.

Having been homeless, Mark has a deep-felt understanding of what it means to be voiceless and powerless. Homeless people are our untouchables. And even though Mark has managed to pull his life back together emotionally and financially, he fully understands how important it is that he make his voice heard and enable others to be heard as well.

Mark helps people living on the street in Los Angeles find shelter. He enables them to tell their own stories on *InvisiblePeopleTV*. Mark also ensures that other Los Angelenos and his online friends are more aware of the plight of homeless people, and gives them important and meaningful ways to help. Mark instinctively understands the opportunity for and importance of Matterness. Mark leads fearlessly, using social media as vehicles for ensuring that everyone in his ecosystem can speak and be heard.

Matterness is the shared space between people and organizations where each is heard, their unique needs are met, and a greater whole is formed. Matterness is:

- The willingness and ability of individuals to speak and be heard;
- The willingness of organizations to listen and work *with* — not *at* — people, and to engage people on the inside and outside as creative problem solvers and ambassadors;
- The smart use of social media to connect people online and on land in huge ecosystems of people

and organizations that are filled with generosity and capital.

In the euphoric first stages of the social media revolution, individuals reveled in their newfound freedom from music companies, newspapers, political parties, expensive retailers, and traditional advocacy organizations. We were suddenly living in a disaggregated, disrupted, digitally powered world, where starting businesses, movements, or revolutions could happen quickly and inexpensively outside of the structures and strictures of traditional organizations.

But there were clearly limitations to what individuals could do alone, as stalled revolutions and causes, unsustainable start-ups, and isolated businesses showed. We still need businesses to manufacture and sell goods, government agencies to ensure civility, and nonprofits to strive for social justice. No matter how many people of goodwill are connected to one another, we still need entities with rules and boundaries to enable people to work together efficiently and generate more resources within their ecosystems. We still need organizations— but we need them to be different and better.

In an ecosystem where a story can go instantly viral, where a shoe store is now competing against many online choices, where there are dozens of environmental causes asking for donations, it is remarkable how hard many organizations work to make their own people feel insignificant and powerless.

Focusing on Matterness enables organizations to create a different kind of internal culture, one that is less afraid to step out into the world, more interested in engaging with people inside and outside of their walls, and more willing to listen to and learn from people. All of these constructive conversations, this collective feeling of being heard and valued, will generate a greater sense of civility, where individuals and their ideas and efforts matter more in the world, where bullies are pulled out of the shadows and confronted, and where common purpose trumps private interests.

It is the *absence* of Matterness that we most often notice — tone-deaf organizations working *at* people rather than *with* them, resulting in either enraged or disinterested constituents. Rather than take the historic opportunity to remake their relationship with their constituents, too many organizations have doubled down on their command-and-control habits. In *The Networked Nonprofit,* Beth Kanter and I called these organizations "fortresses," meaning that they are bureaucratic on the inside, opaque and mysterious from the outside. As a result, a standoff has developed, with people taking to their social media channels to yell, *"J'accuse!"* when organizations fail them, and organizations crouched behind their fortress walls, unwilling and unable to engage with the world in open and honest ways.

The lack of Matterness contributes to:

- *Organizations routinely turning a deaf ear to customer concerns.* Organizations routinely ignore customer-service data and feedback, even the feedback they intentionally solicit. John Goodman studied customer service for over thirty years, from the 1970s past the millennium. The patterns and results remained remarkably the same over the decades. Goodman estimates that 95% of complaints are either unreported or reported to a front-line representative who is unlikely to accurately represent the complaint due to self-preservation. Organizations develop defense mechanisms to guard against criticism, in the same way as individuals. It is painful to be called names or deemed worthless; therefore, people, and the organizations in which they work, develop specific strategies for avoiding criticism. This means that top-level managers hear only 5% of all the complaints about their organization. A decline in reported complaints, therefore, is not necessarily a sign of improved service but more often tied to "trained helplessness," the feeling on the part of constituents that no one cares about them or their concerns.

The reality is that most people are not comfortable complaining. But when they summon the courage to complain, they expect, and deserve, to be listened to and acknowledged. In the long run, a sincere apology goes a long way towards turning a complainer into a loyal customer. This is enormously important to organizations in an economy drive by reputation.

- *Organizations continue to talk* at *rather than* with *their constituents.* Unhappy customers generally tell twice as many people about their experience as happy customers. Except on social media, where they tell four times as many people. And yet, an overwhelming number of organizations use social media only as newfangled billboards rather than opportunities to listen and talk with constituents. For instance, nearly 75% of respondents to a national survey of nonprofit organizations report using social media as a megaphone for broadcasting messages rather than building online communities. A 2011 study by Martiz Research and evolve24 found that over 70% of customer complaints by Twitter were ignored by companies.

- *The mistrust of institutions continues unabated.* Every year since 2001, the public relations firm Edelman has released a broad and far-reaching survey to measure public trust across industries and institutions worldwide. The public views business as mediocre at best when it comes to trustworthiness, and government fares far worse. Congress has a lower approval rating today than at any other time in the eighty-year history of Gallup polls.

- *The flat-lining of public well-being.* No single indicator of American well-being has improved significantly over the last several decades. Adjusted for inflation, incomes for most Americans have flattened or fallen over the past several decades. Billions of dollars spent by government and nonprofits on school-reform efforts, public health, housing, and job training have failed to improve outcomes in any area.

- *Stop energy trumps go energy.* "Stop energy" are the episodes of outrage that a video or policy shared via social media elicit. "Go energy" is collective problem solving. As Micah Sifry writes, "...in an environment of increasingly dispersed attention, the Internet is much better at gathering 'stop' energy than it is at building 'go' energy."

The purpose of this book is to provide a framework for understanding why Matterness is so important to both people and organizations and to provide guidance for organizational leaders on how to incorporate Matterness as a fundamental part of their efforts. This framework focuses on the three essential components of Matterness:

- **The Opportunity for Every Person to Play Multiple Roles.** We each play a wide variety of roles at any given moment in our ecosystems. At any moment in time, inside or outside of organizations, each one of us can be givers, receivers, donors, buyers, or sharers. And, in the biggest shift, sometimes people and organizations are leaders, and sometimes they are followers.

- **Leverages Our Fundamentally Social Nature.** We cannot matter sitting alone in our rooms. We have to engage with other people on land and online in order to count and be heard. In so doing, our best traits of generosity, empathy, and kindness emerge, which science shows us empirically leads directly to happiness. Sitting on the sidelines, voiceless and powerless, leads to feelings of rage, frustration, cynicism, and defeat. Organizations — and the people who lead them — can choose to keep us at a distance, frustrating our desire to matter, or they can engage us in satisfying ways that turn us into long-term customers and supporters. And this leads to the final point....

- **Matterness Requires Leadership.** A different kind of leadership is necessary to make Matterness the norm within organizations. Leadership that enhances Matterness is open to the input of constituents, encourages leaders to be human beings with real flaws and vulnerabilities, values relationships over transactions, and is a capable facilitator of crowds of people with their own good ideas and resources.

It became clear to me how painful the absence of Matterness is for people when I began my tenure as president of my synagogue a few years ago. The first reaction from congregants when I assumed my role was: "Congratulations!" The second was a litany of complaints by email. "Dear Madam President: My parking spot was taken." "The doors were locked when I arrived for my meeting." "I didn't get a timely thank-you note." "My name was misspelled on a letter."

Naturally, I rolled up my sleeves and began to respond to each complaint individually. I made sure the doors were open when they were supposed to be. New signs about the parking spaces were installed. Thank-you letters were sent more quickly. And then I received this complaint: "I was in the hospital last week, and no one called — even though I didn't tell anyone I was sick."

This complaint was so absurd and nonsensical that it made me stop and ask myself, "What in the world is going on here?"

It wasn't just the number of complaints I received but the intensity of them that took me aback. People were furious about relatively minor problems. And then I looked around and saw these kinds of complaints everywhere: The couple yelling at the hostess for not holding their dinner reservation. *But we come here all the time — we're regulars!* The man watching his personal physician scan a chart furiously, trying to figure out who the shivering person sitting in a paper-towel gown in front of her is. The donors who finally give up on a cause they have donated to for years because their last name has been misspelled over and over again. The company representative asking for the ID code *they* use to identify clients and acting indignant when you can't find it. The pastor who still doesn't know his parishioner's name after ten years at the church. The store employee who can't be bothered to greet a customer.

This feeling of personal diminishment is perfectly summed up by the urban legend of the Publisher's Clearinghouse Sweepstakes addressed to Mr. Roman C. Archbishop of Boston. *Congratulations, Mr. Archbishop — You May Have Just Won $1 Million!*

These are all fundamentally the same complaint: I thought you cared about me, and you don't. I thought I was more important to you than a stranger off the street. But sadly, it feels like I am just a name, a data point, an address, a checkbook. In other words: I don't matter. Maya Angelou wrote, "I've learned that people will forget what you said, people will forget what you did, but people will never forget the way you made them feel." Understanding and incorporating Matterness into our lives is the way to ensure that people and organizations bring out the best in each other.

About this Book

This book describes how each one of us can lead in such a way that people around us matter more. It is not a prescription but a general guide, with many pathways forward. Every person is responsible for choosing her own way ahead.

The issues and lessons discussed in this book cut across every sector of the economy and every kind of organization, from corporations to nonprofits to government agencies. It can get very confusing using different words, including "companies," "agencies," "institutions," "organizations," and "social networks" to express the same idea — an entity where people work together for a common purpose.

In addition, organizations are less distinct from each other based on sector than ever before: Corporations are incorporating social responsibility into their efforts, nonprofits look and act more like corporations, and government agencies regularly incorporate principles, practices, and structures from the other two sectors. In light of both the possibility for confusion and the blending of institutional types, I've chosen to use one word, *organization,* to mean all of those things and hope the context will make it clear if I mean an entity within a particular sector of the economy.

I use the word *constituent* to mean all of the people who can participate in shaping an organization's culture and agenda — if the organization lets them. Constituents live and work in an ecosystem of other people and organizations. "Social networks" is often used to describe these ecosystems, however, I chose the word *ecosystem* deliberately for this book because it better conveys the humanity of the sphere, rather than the technology of it.

Any work trying to make sense of societal patterns will provide easy fodder for those who want to point out the exceptions. For instance, it is easy to point out that some people are mean and greedy; but most people aren't, nor is it the way we are wired to behave. And some people's personal experiences have been so searing — perhaps they were mugged at one time, or were bullied online, or worked for a mean-spirited boss — that they cannot see clearly enough to recognize that, most of the time, the intentions and experiences of other people and institutions is positive.

The Organization of This Book

This book begins with *The Tyranny of Dichotomy,* which addresses and undoes the assumptions holding us back from appreciating and understanding where and how we can matter. It is followed by *Living in Big Small Towns,* a description of the combined space online and on land in which we are living.

The section on "Managing Matterness" includes two chapters. *Working From the Inside Out* outlines why organizations work at a distance from their constituents. This chapter includes discussion of "The Churn" — the inward gravitational pull of work away from constituents and toward process-focused to-do lists. *Leading From the Outside In* outlines how to reverse and engage people on the outside as active shapers, not passive bystanders, for organizations.

The following section, "Scaling Matterness," has three chapters. *Scaling Matterness Within Organizations* explains how to work with the agility to match the fast change of ecosystems without getting sucked into The Churn. *Using Crowds to Scale Matterness* describes the different types of capital available to organizations now, but only if leaders understand what kinds of help they need. *Action Cascades of Matterness* provides leadership advice for plugging into and steering in a positive direction the crowds that may be activated to help your organization.

The final chapter is *A Call for Collective Responsibility*— the ways we need to live and work together, and ways that online-platform providers need to ensure that our commons remain balanced between their private needs and our common interests.

The Tyranny of Dichotomy

THERE IS A SET OF ASSUMPTIONS about the way the world is organized and operates are barriers to Matterness. We developed these notions that define people and society as a suit of armor for protection in the last century, but, now, they are holding us back. For instance, if leaders assume that people are naturally mean spirited, it becomes impossible for the organization to wholeheartedly reach out to the world and ask for help. *Real* help, as in: *How do we create safe spaces for teens to hang out together,* not *fake* help as in: *Your $25 will solve hunger in America today.* When these assumptions stop people and organizations from engaging with people in open and constructive ways, the tyranny of dichotomous thinking has taken hold.

Dichotomous thinking is the all-or-nothing approach to life, a zero-sum game that locks people into extreme positions. When we believe our lives are sorted into "this or that" — that people can be only good or bad, or that an environment can be only safe or dangerous — we don't know how to engage with the world differently when the truth — that the world is neither all good nor all bad — appears. If a house gets robbed, it does not mean that the entire neighborhood is dangerous, and if one troll slams your organization on Yelp, it does not mean that the entire Internet is mean spirited.

The areas of dichotomous thinking that keep us from fully embracing the notion of and need for Matterness need to be taken out into the sunlight and examined in order for us to move collectively to a more productive place. Leaving them unchallenged stops us from imagining, much less realizing, a world where people can speak and be heard and successfully share, co-create, and live together. These assumptions are that: 1) people are naturally mean and greedy, 2) we are living in a particularly dangerous society, and 3) technology is stopping us from being civil to one another.

This chapter will examine each one of these assumptions and how to re-imagine them in order to put Matterness at the center of life and work.

False Assumption #1: People Are Naturally Mean and Greedy

Leo Durocher, the legendary manager of the Brooklyn Dodgers, never actually said, "Nice guys finish last." Still, people want to believe that he did, *and* they want to believe that it is true. The assumption that we are mean and greedy is the perfect leitmotif in the narratives of people and businesses determined not to be suckers. In reality, however, we are naturally kind and are ready to help other people and organizations, often with nothing but emotional satisfaction in return.

Matterness exists in the interaction between organizations and people. If that space is filled with the presumption that people are mean and greedy, the interaction is colored by suspicion — if not automatically doomed to failure. Social media provide an opportunity for everyday acts of kindness and generosity to be captured and shared widely — and yet, many people still refuse to believe that it is our natural state of being.

Our predisposition to kindness and generosity begins with our tribal origins. Some members of the tribe farmed, some hunted, some raised children, some cooked. Being tribal requires cooperation to be successful. The resources they created through individual tasks were shared.

The Hadza is a tribe of hunter-gatherers living in Tanzania who have been untouched by modern influences or industrialization. They exhibit all of the traditional characteristics of a tribal society. They also have social networks, with some people exhibiting more influence than others. For instance, individual Hadza who name more friends are also named as friends more frequently by others. These influential people are even claimed as friends by people they barely know. People who resemble each other in some physical way tend to be connected as well; for Hadza people, similarity in age, body fat, and handgrip strength increases the likelihood of friendship.

The social ties that people have anywhere in the world mimic those fundamental social ties and patterns of the Hadza tribe. A recent study found that the number of social connections a person has is remarkably similar across groups living around the world. Whether one is looking at schoolyards in the Midwest, at a rural community in Romania, or at entrepreneurs in Miami Beach, the basic nature of social networks continues to hold true.

No matter what kinds of technologies are enabling us to connect with other people, we continue to be homophilous, meaning we flock with other birds who think and look like us. People have between four and six close relationships, on average. Connections between people in our tribes are strengthened by acts of generosity and kindness. We continue to live and act like the Hazda because it makes us feel good, safe, and productive.

People who are kind and generous are also happy. In fact, research shows that almost any act of kindness boosts happiness. In one study, a group of 9-to-11-year-old kids were asked to do acts of kindness for several weeks. The results were that, "not only did they get happier over time, but they became more popular with their peers." The cool kids are the kind ones! In addition, the recipients of kindness "paid the kind acts forward," and because kindness is contagious, even acquaintances of the givers became happier and were inspired to act more generously.

Two studies supported by the National Institutes of Health reported that, when people act in altruistic ways, their brain activates areas that experience joy. This is what the researcher James Andreoni calls "Warm-Glow Giving." The motivation doesn't matter; it simply feels good to give someone something. And, more than producing good feelings on the inside, it makes the giver more attractive to others on the outside. Altruism not only enhances our status within the tribe, it makes us more attractive to the opposite sex, increasing a person's likelihood of finding a mate and reproducing. Givers are sex magnets!

Americans are amazingly generous people. In 2011, Americans gave $298.42 billion to charities. We created the modern practice of institutional philanthropy; we volunteer in larger numbers and for more time than the citizens of any other country in the world. We give willingly and enthusiastically to an overwhelming number of causes that range from religious and educational institutions to social causes, animal rights, the environment, political campaigns, and advocacy efforts.

We give rationally to people and institutions we know personally, say, a college, and causes, like diseases, that affect us personally. We also give irrationally to people we don't know and causes that don't affect us directly—and we still feel better because of it.

Giving to causes in which you have no personal connection to the affected parties, over which you have no personal oversight as to how the funds are used, where the outcomes are uncertain, and where the impact of your $25 is miniscule only makes sense if one understands an area of behavioral ecology called Costly Signaling Theory. This theory explains why individuals are generous and kind to others without any monetary or material benefit to themselves. Public generosity signals to others that we are kind people, from which one can infer that we are good mates. An influential paper by Tamas Bereczkei, Bela Birkas, and Zsuzsanna Kerekes entitled "Altruism Toward Strangers in Need: Costly Signaling in an Industrial Society" explains altruism toward strangers. They write, "Thus, public generosity can be seen as a form of competition among men that increases their reproductive success in terms of getting sexual partners." We're back to sex, or, more accurately, we're back to survival of the tribe, which happens when our best and most generous selves are exhibited.

Generosity extends to networking platforms like LinkedIn that are overflowing with advice givers, job recommenders, and people connecters. This is not just because the job recommender today becomes the job seeker tomorrow in an economy where employment lasts on average just three years, but because generosity feels good and enhances the status of the giver. The same feel-good chemical oxytocin that is released in your brain when you help a disabled elderly person cross the street is also released when you introduce a graphic designer to the owner of a web firm in your network. One study found that individuals helped strangers in their networks — even with no guarantee that the act would be appreciated or reciprocated — because it enhanced their own reputations.

We have the largest public commons in the history of the world online where every day, without fanfare or recognition, billions of people are acting kindly and generously. Social media have not made us kinder and more generous, rather, they provide many more avenues to easily and public express and share our kindnesses.

We "Like" what other people say and do online. We want to acknowledge their joy, sorrow, hardship, and express sympathy for the everyday annoyances of life. We may still drive into our garages and walk into our houses and turn on our TVs, but in the time that we have done so, twelve other people may have clicked "Like" on the news of a promotion or the birth of a baby or sent words of condolence for a pet that just passed way. We are no longer alone. These expressions of comfort and friendship can be an end in themselves — one, simple act of loving kindness — or they can begin a rippling tide of expressions of empathy and actions. The results are cascades of kindness explored further in Chapter Seven.

False Assumption #2: Society Is Particularly Dangerous

Millions of people are gathering the courage to connect with new people online and on land to share a passion or organize an event or create a new club. Since people are naturally kind and generous, then comfortably engaging with each other should feel natural. However, the second false assumption — that our society is particularly dangerous — often stops us from trying. People cannot participate fully in society and with organizations, and organizations cannot open themselves up to their constituents with all of our wonderful gifts of empathy and caring, because they are locked behind closed doors.

The rate of crime, particularly per capita in our fast-growing country, has actually gone down over the past thirty years. In 1980, there were slightly more than 23,000 murders committed in the United States. In 2010, there were 14,772. There were 27% more people in the United States during that time, meaning that the murder rate per person in the United States had dropped by more than 50%. In Maine, there were 32 murders in 1980 and 26 in 2010, more than 13,000 burglaries in 1980 and 7,364 in 2010. But largely rural Maine may not be a representative example. Let's take a hard one — how about Los Angeles County? In 1980, there were a total of 51,448 violent crimes committed. In 2010, there were 21,241.

There continue to be stubborn pockets of intense poverty and violence. If you live in parts of Detroit, East Baltimore, or East St. Louis, the onslaught of drugs and crime continues to overwhelm life. In addition, the incarceration of young African American men is a largely unrecognized national tragedy. But outside of those pockets, where the vast majority of Americans live, we are much safer than we were thirty years ago — we just don't believe that we are. It's possible that there has been a national underreporting of violent crime taking place over the past thirty years. But that's not probable. What is much more likely is that our fear of violent crime is out of proportion with the reality of it.

There are two factors fueling our outsized fear of violent crime. The first is that bad news is far stickier than good news and that the sharing of horrific stories of violence and incivility are staples of news media. The daily drumbeat of violence and incivility that saturates news reports creates a national state of tension and fear. *Your local high school with marauding gangs of boys raping girls — tune in for the 5 o'clock news for more! Crackheads setting a whistleblower's house on fire, video at eleven!* We are bombarded by messages about crime, violence, and stranger-danger.

Social media turn these local stories into national news, spreading the conventional wisdom of the awfulness of society. The nationalization of news traumatizes the rest of us watching from afar. Scenes from school shootings unfold over and again online and in the media. The trauma is real even if the reality is that violence in and around schools has plummeted since 1992. Any chance that an armed madman could go to your child's elementary school and start shooting everyone in sight creates a gnawing fear in the pit of every parent's stomach, regardless of the likelihood of that happening.

The second factor supporting our outsized fear of violent crime is that we are living in a stressful and anxious economic time that makes bad news resonate loudly. Long-term unemployment has become a chronic problem for millions of people, corporate loyalty is a long-gone notion, and pensions and retirement accounts seem quaint. Everyone is working longer hours for the same pay, and social media have made us constantly "on" and available as an expectation, not an exception. Most Americans are living in a fixed and regular state of anxiety, with mountains of college debt, a house underwater, aging parents, and no pension funds. Life feels like a constant, exhausting battle to stay afloat financially and emotionally.

Income inequality is real and entrenched. From the mid 1920s to World War II, the top one-percenters earned around 45 percent of total income. After World War II, which was, not coincidentally, during our country's period of greatest strength domestically and internationally, the top one percent earned just above 32.5 percent of total income and stayed about there until the 1970s. The top one percent in 2012 "...is equal to 50.4 percent, a level higher than any other year since 1917 and even surpasses 1928, the peak of the stock market bubble in the 'roaring' 1920s." Not even the Great Recession could put a permanent dent in these numbers. From 2009 to 2011, the income of the top 1% dropped dramatically, by 17.4%; however, for the two years afterwards, the top 1% grew by 31.4%, while bottom 99% incomes grew only by 0.4% from 2009 to 2012.

Along with a growing gap between rich and poor, we also aren't socializing across socio-economic borders as we once did. There was a time when people mixed, regardless of income, at church, at public school board meetings, at the Rotary Club. Those opportunities don't exist anymore, as rich and poor people aren't melding, mixing, or even bumping into one another. This is why the existence of "Google buses," the fleet of private buses that take San Franciscans into the mountains to work at Google, Facebook, Apple, Entertainment Arts, and Genentech, is such a sore spot in a city renowned for its egalitarianism.

Our natural inclination to be kind and generous easily disappears in stressful economic environments. Stress creates a lens through which we view our world as mean-spirited, one that requires ruthlessness and self-protection for survival, even if that isn't a true picture of the world or its inhabitants.

It is heroic to be able to retain a fundamental sense of humanity under awful circumstances. And, yet, some remarkable people like Nelson Mandela, who was imprisoned by a totalitarian state for twenty-seven years for his political beliefs, manage to do so. For most people, however, when the strain from physical fear or economic anxiety becomes too high, then being mean or greedy becomes rational — or, at least, rationalized.

The strains of everyday life have put us on high alert at all times, ready for battle. Imagine this scenario: You leave your house for work in the morning. A neighbor waves to you as you get into your car, and you smile and wave back. You arrive at Starbucks for your daily latte at the exact same time as someone you don't know. "Go ahead of me," she says, "I'm not really in a hurry to get to work!" You both laugh. You ask your regular Starbucks barista how his weekend went and banter back and forth for a minute before the mutter of impatient caffeine-hounds behind you tells you to move on. Your coffee in hand, you start your drive to work. You are singing loudly and off key to Coldplay when a guy in a red Alfa Romeo cuts you off. You slam on your brakes, honk your horn and yell "Idiot!" He looks directly at you, smiles, and gives you the finger. He speeds up and weaves in front of the next car, causing it to slam on his brakes, and disappears ahead. It's outrageous, his rudeness, his dangerous driving! Why isn't there a cop around when you need one? Why doesn't anything bad ever happen to jerks who are so rude and dangerous?

Which interaction are you more likely to share with your co-workers when you get to work? Which one shapes your mood? Which one elicits responses from others like, "People are ***so*** rude today!" And, yet there were three pleasant, polite, nice interactions to the one rude one. Why does the rude one outweigh all the others? Because our brains are wired for survival, ensuring that we pay heightened attention to environmental threats.

The fear of society, unfortunately, also makes us overly wary of strangers. We are literally surrounded by people we don't know because, on average, Americans move fourteen different times and hold eleven different jobs over their lifetimes. Nearly a quarter of the population of the country has moved in the last five years. In fact, the only people in the world who move more often than we do are people living in war-torn countries.

Who are all of these wanderers? Some have moved for new jobs. More are fresh college graduates (who have grown from a quarter to a third of the college-age people over the last forty years) coming to town with a shiny new degree, a mountain of debt, and, probably, few social ties. When we are surrounded by strangers, rather than lifelong family and friends, it makes society seem more unfriendly.

Of course, real dangers exist. People do unimaginably terrible things every day. There are bullies, rapists, murderers, pedophiles, and just plain creeps. Yik Yak, an anonymous chat board, enables people to say horrible things about people they know, taking gossip from whispers to shouts. And, stupid people do stupid things to hurt themselves and other people every day. More than an ounce of common sense and decency is needed to navigate safely in this world, and, sadly, not all of us have even that much. But these people are the exception, and there are certainly not enough of them to warrant keeping ourselves locked behind our doors.

Allowing the fear of strangers and societal chaos and violence to isolate us is a choice, not a necessity. For instance, Steve Jobs and Bill Gates were both born in 1955. Jobs grew up in Silicon Valley and Gates in Seattle, in middle-class and upper-middle-class neighborhoods, respectively. When their fortunes and families grew, they chose how they wanted to live. Gates built a 66,000-square-foot mansion near Seattle for his wife and three children, literally a fortress with high walls and security guards for protection. Jobs bought an unpretentious house in Old Palo Alto for his wife and three kids. The neighborhood was wealthy, no doubt, but the houses weren't hidden from view, there were wide sidewalks, and he never had a security detail for protection. And he never had a problem. Jobs' family chose not to live their lives based on the premise that something could possibly go wrong.

Choosing to shut out the world is as counterproductive for organizations as it is for individuals. Fearing the world and the uncontrollable people populating it to the point where it makes more sense to withdraw and keep the doors closed rather than open makes embracing Matterness nearly impossible.

False Assumption #3: Social Media Are Making Us Less Civil.

Matterness is not powered by any one social media tool but by the entire social media toolset, with its common characteristics of being digitally powered, relatively easy to use, and astoundingly easy to share information. The false assumption that social media are making us less civil invalidates the online ecosystems' overwhelming reach and power for good.

Social media have two characteristics that contribute to their fundamental role in reshaping society and their importance in increasing Matterness. The first is that we can choose to be known to more people online. We can have a more-well-known face, name, and voice in the wider digital world than we could in the analog world. We can easily take actions like sharing information, making new friends, and chronicling life at a speed and scale never before experienced.

The second characteristic is the conversational nature of social media. Social media aren't one-way broadcast media controlled by companies. Using social media, anyone can say anything at any time to anyone. Organizations can use social media to participate in free-flowing conversations with their constituents, but, sadly, as mentioned previously, too many organizations continue to sit behind their fortress walls and use social media as online billboards and commercials.

It is these two characteristics — the ability to have our voices carry further and the potentially chaotic nature of uncontrolled conversations — that can also make social media feel like the driver of incivility.

Often, a dinner-party conversation about social media boils down into two dichotomous views: "Social media are the panacea for all social ills," or "Social media are the driver of all social ills." Neither position is correct. Social media didn't create communities or social networks or the desire to connect and share with one another. They have made all of those things visible, easier, faster, cheaper — and bigger. Social media don't make people mean or narcissistic — they enable mean and narcissistic people to have a bigger platform for sharing their feelings.

The idea that social media are destroying personal relationships is born from the false notion that there is a "real" world on land versus an "artificial" world online. In fact, most of us are so accustomed to assuming that life takes place either online or on land — another example of dichotomous thinking — that we don't realize we're making a false assumption. For instance, here is a recent conversation I had with my husband, a very savvy and successful technologist:

Me:	I'm writing about living in one big space. One that isn't online or on land but an integrated whole.
Husband:	Of course, I get that. I have my regular friends and my Facebook friends.
Me:	No, you don't get it...dear. That's exactly what I'm saying we *don't* have anymore. We just have friends, wherever we bump into them.
Husband:	That doesn't make any sense. If I have just met someone on Facebook, how can they be as good a friend as my best buddy from high school?
Me:	They can't be, but it's not because of Facebook—you just don't have enough social capital built up between you and the new person yet. You don't have any shared memories, and you don't trust one another enough to fully reveal yourself yet. But it could easily be the reverse. You could connect with a high school buddy on Facebook and continue to strengthen your already-deep relationship and have a new acquaintance at the gym (you remember that place?) or at the coffee shop.
Husband:	(muttering under his breath but easily audible) That makes sense.... She Who Must Be Obeyed....
Me:	Go pick up the kids.

We are living online *and* on land at the same time, not in one space or the other, but in both spaces together, simultaneously. Alice Marwick, a scholar on social media, said, "The separation [of online and on-land communities] is artificial. Trying to look at them as separate is hard and complicated. What we do online influences offline, and vice versa." Whatever we do anywhere is our real world, and what we feel and know carries over to any other place or space we occupy. There is no evidence, no data, no research that proves that we are different people when socializing online versus on land. We are who we are wherever we are.

Online connections are easy ways to stay in touch with past friends, acquaintances, and business connections. We now have opportunities to bump into people we would not ordinarily see during the course of a regular day. Social media stretch our notion of friends and community, but they don't redefine them. We can feel a sense of intimacy with people online and then go to the supermarket and feel distant and removed from the people right around us. Social media aren't making relationships better or worse — they are simply creating connections. What we choose to do with those connections is up to each one of us.

Matterness creates both the opportunity and the responsibility for being accountable to one another for what we say and do. The opposite is also true: People can be held responsible for things that they say and do that they wish would go away.

Anonymity is a complicated issue. Anonymity is critically important in certain environments like Alcoholics Anonymous. Political protesters in tyrannical countries need anonymity to organize, and whistleblowers need it in the workplace. Choosing to be anonymous to cause others pain, though, should not be allowed to outweigh our collective need for civility. We have space within our common humanity to be both known and unknown; however, civility depends on more of us being known to one another.

Because individual voices carry quickly, widely, and inexpensively around the Web, incivility spreads very easily. Bullying and uncivil behavior exist online, and hoaxes, cons, catfishing, identity theft, and misinformation exist. The mean-spirited thoughts of one person that would before have stayed between that person and their diary or a small group of in-person friends or the beleaguered editor of the local newspaper are now posted and visible for the rest of us to have to endure. Formerly private craziness can now be turned into public vitriol. And seemingly innocuous events can turn into enormous conflagrations.

Social media bring out the best in most of us and, sadly, make visible the worst in some of us. They make the unpleasant thoughts and actions of individuals spread easily for the rest of us to see, in real time, without any filters.

We will never be able to eliminate society's darkest corners entirely. And, sadly, in the same way that most people want to matter in order to have their smart opinions and talents recognized, a smaller segment of people want to matter by expressing hatred. However, misplacing the blame on the tools instead of the standard of behavioral expectation reinforces the false assumption that technology is making us uncivil. Technology doesn't send messages — people do, and most of us are perfectly civil (and kind and generous) online.

We need a broad commitment to enforcing civility online that wasn't necessary when the Net was new and not the backbone of our social and economic lives. It is up to each one of us to defend our online communities against the small pockets of people who behave otherwise. Although the Web was born as a Libertarian playground, given the central role it now plays in all of our lives, it now requires a new culture. Just because incivility has found a welcome home on the Internet does not mean that the rest of us have to accept it as inevitable or unstoppable. It is every person's responsibility to uphold and to insist on civility online in the same way we would on land.

We need to protect spaces online where wonderful things can happen, where civil people can congregate and exchange views without vitriol. We need to actively call out bad behavior too often excused as "boys being boys" or people acting badly behind their anonymous screen names. We need to come to the rescue of people who are unfairly targeted for hate. We need to encourage schools to facilitate thoughtful discussions about how to productively live online rather than the fearful way they most often talk about the Web *("Join us on Tuesday to discuss all the ways the Internet is ruining your child!")*

Some online social platforms are actively working to promote greater civility. On Everyblock, a website to connect neighbors, an "unneighborly" button exists to make it clear when someone has crossed a line from complaining to attacking. YouTube, previously a magnet for horrid behavior by commenters, has created a series of filters and controls for video creators to use to block trolls and particular words from the comment section.

We cannot hide from incivility and cruelty, but we can thoughtfully engage with the world as it is without becoming so restrictive that we cut ourselves off from the benefits of living online. The need for a widespread insistence on civility is too important to wait for organizations to do the hard work alone; individuals need to establish and enforce this new culture in our own spheres. We need an online civility pledge. Here is a draft intended to begin a conversation for a short, simple set of ways we need to behave together online:

1. **Words matter.** Since 90% of human communications are non-verbal, the intent of words absent the body and voice of the writer can be easily misunderstood. Words need to be chosen carefully to convey the true meeting of the writer. Because

it can be so difficult to understand the intent of a writer online, emoticons and symbols should be used often to convey the feelings of the writer.

2. **Don't Just Watch.** According to the 18th-century philosopher Edmund Burke, "Evil wins when good men do nothing." Too many of us are watching incivility and not doing enough about it. Perhaps it has to do with the origins of the Web as a rough-and-tumble space, but it's no longer an excuse to do nothing. We need to defend one another and the civil space we are trying to create with vigor. We need to come to the defense of victims quickly, publicly, and energetically.

3. **The Stranger Test.** Anyone considering sending out a smart-ass message should write it and then stop. Now imagine saying the same thing to a stranger on the street, someone who didn't know your sense of humor. If the stranger isn't offended, you're good to go.

4. **Pay It Forward.** We, the consumers, customers, donors, and volunteers, are obliged to pay it forward when something good happens as part of the community compact. We can't just be complainers — we also have to be celebrators. Tell the world that your server was just lovely and friendly. Tweet how good it felt when the store not only took your item back with no questions asked but helped you find something new. Scan and post that lovely hand-written thank-you note from the environmental cause.

Conclusion

The greatest danger to our society comes from the continuation of dichotomous thinking. How we see the world we live in affects the choices we make about whether and how to engage in it and with whom. We could choose to wall ourselves off and live only at lightning speed, self-absorbed and unwilling to work together to build a better society. Or we could choose to unlock our doors and appreciate the fact that people are naturally and overwhelmingly kind and generous and want to help other people. We have an opportunity to recapture the fundamental humanness that makes us empathetic, kind, and creative. Living this way can provide a foundation for building an equitable and just society.

Discussion Questions

- Where in your life have you been prone to dichotomous thinking?
- What assumptions about people in general may you need to challenge and, perhaps, undo?
- How are your social assumptions affecting your work and life? Are your windows and doors closed, open just a crack, or wide open? Could they be open differently?

2

Living in Big Small Towns

I GREW UP IN Sleepy Hollow, New York. Yes, *that* Sleepy Hollow — with the famous cemetery and the Old Dutch Church with its stained-glass windows painted by the artist Marc Chagall. The majestic Hudson River was outside our window, and the Headless Horseman was still roaming about, at least according to rumor. In a village of fewer than 10,000 people, we had a mayor and village trustees (one of which I would become when I was 21, a long story for a different book), our own fire and police departments, a local bank, and a local newspaper. Most of the villagers were descendants of Italian immigrants who arrived in the early 20th century to build John D. Rockefeller's palatial estate, Kykuit. My family moved there when I was nine, but I always felt just a little bit like an outsider for not having been born there.

Today, the village looks very much like it did in the 1970s and 80s. The main street still dead-ends at the

Hudson River, which is actually much cleaner than when I grew up swimming in it. The cemetery is the same, and so is the church. But significant changes have occurred in Sleepy Hollow.

The local newspaper was bought by the Gannett chain in 1998 and incorporated into a countywide paper. A regional bank acquired the Sleepy Hollow Bank in 2008.

The General Motors manufacturing plant, the largest manufacturer in New York State, closed in 1986. After decades of litigation that enriched scores of lawyers, the site was finally transformed into a hive of luxury condominiums located a short walk from the train station to speed commuters twenty miles south to New York City. There has also been an enormous influx of Hispanic residents, some legal, more not. These changes resulted in a population increase, according to the U. S. Census Bureau, from 8,152 people in 1990 to 9,870 in 2010, a 17% rise.

One result of all of these changes was that it became more common to be from somewhere else, to be a newcomer to Sleepy Hollow rather than a native. In other words, more people were unknown to one another and Matterness couldn't grow.

At the end of the last century, we were a nation having a mid-life crisis. Instead of buying fancy sports cars, we sat on our couches watching broadcast media telling us what to do and think. We became disassociated from local communities and clubs. Our jobs became more insecure than ever as they were shipped overseas or squeezed out by technological advances. We were uprooted from our hometowns, unknown to one another, insecure, and, well, a little bit lonely.

It was inevitable, many people felt, that small towns like Sleepy Hollow — and certainly the sprawling mega-urban communities around the country — were destined to become anonymous and atomized places, with people living near one another but separate, alone, and apart.

But in that moment, unbeknownst to most people, we had already started a new epoch in human social development. With the advent of the World Wide Web and easy access to commercial email in the early 1990s, we were instantly talking to anyone, anywhere, at any time, and at little cost. The social web followed, with new ways for individuals to connect with one another and re-connect with old friends.

We began to Recombobulate. Our small towns morphed into something new and different: Big Small Towns. Big Small Towns are the sum of on-land and online communities that combine the intimacy and caring of old-fashioned towns with the ease of connections, expansiveness, and never-ending resources of the Internet. Most importantly, Big Small Towns enable people to be what they are intended to be: Connected, caring, curious, and capable.

Today, anyone living in the Big Small Town of Sleepy Hollow can easily connect with other people who are interested in attachment parenting, kayaking, wedding and event planning, motorcycling, meditation, single lesbians, the Tea Party, ballroom dancing, or photography and can easily find other local people with the same interests using a website like Meetup. A Facebook group called 10591, the local zip code, enables residents to update one another with school news, announcements, and complaints. There is a local news website called Patch that provides a variety of local news, including updates from the police crime blotter, school news, celebrations of accomplishments like a new book published by a local resident or a new art display at the library. Yelp and Angie's

List provide recommendations for restaurants, plumbers, and many local stores. There are bloggers keeping residents updated on school news and local developments. People are buying and selling used furniture on Craigslist and announcing tag sales, too.

Matterness thrives and expands in Big Small Towns, in which people express (or overexpress!) their opinions, help one another find resources or navigate systems, force local governments to listen to complaints, and celebrate life's events together. Big Small Towns are not so much geographic places as much as spaces that combine the power and reach of online and on-land communities. The story of the Mom Bloggers Club later in this chapter illustrates a Big Small Town that exists largely online and extends around the world. More important than the geographic base of a Big Small Town is the fact that its residents are brought together in their on-land and online worlds in empowering ways.

This chapter describes how Big Small Towns operate to increase Matterness, the importance of being known to more people in Big Small Towns, and the gift of social spackling that is knitting Big Small Towns together.

How Big Small Towns Operate

A 2011 study by Facebook found that we had moved from six degrees of separation between any two people in the world to just four with the spread of online social networks like, well, Facebook. However, it is important to note that these connections still have a land-based component, with 93% of Facebook friends reporting that they had met one another in person. We are connected to more people, and are more easily connectable to more people, than ever before.

We have social networks at work, through professional associations, religious congregations, and schools.

All of our connections within these networks can be seen and maintained over time more easily because of social media. Social media enable us to keep up with our next-door neighbor and our friend in Sri Lanka at the same time and with the same amount of energy. And, contrary to what many people believe, the increased use of online social networks not only increases the strength of our existing relationships with other people but actually reduces loneliness.

There is no set formula for how and when we participate on land versus online. We participate in ways that suit our current interests and needs. A caregiver for a spouse with Alzheimer's finds that her group of high school friends on Facebook has become a daily social lifeline. A recent college graduate moving to Atlanta finds a roommate, a health club, restaurant recommendations, and a date through her online networks. A group of parents upset about the quality of school lunches create a petition on Change.org, turning their disorganized group of upset parents into an organized crowd wielding a very large megaphone. When the need is over, the crowd goes home. However, whenever we go offline, we take the ideas, people, and content with us.

In addition to allowing us to participate when we want, social media also enable us to play many different roles in life's unfolding narratives. At any moment in time, a person can be a sharer of news or a commenter regarding another person's news. Anyone can create and share a work of art, ask for help or offer help, organize an event, or participate in someone else's event. We can be leaders and followers, creators and watchers, organizers and doers. One of the greatest assets of living in Big Small Towns is the opportunity to be any one of these things, or all of these things, at any moment in time. This is an incredibly powerful way of living.

Big Small Towns are not just filled with people, of course; they are also filled with organizations. These are no longer stand-alone entities (if they ever truly were) but operate within a much larger ecosystem of other people and organizations. It is critically important for organizational leaders to appreciate that they are not the only or best or most unique dry cleaner/arts organization/grocery store/accounting firm — they are only one of many such entities. The shape and role of organizations are changing rapidly in environments where people have direct access to resources and other people, and no longer necessarily need organizations as brokers or intermediaries.

Traditionally, organizations set their agendas behind closed doors and told the world what they planned to do and what specific, non-negotiable roles their constituents could play in supporting their efforts. They were accustomed to speaking *at,* not *with,* their people. In Big Small Towns, organizations need to focus on their role in relationship to other people and organizations, not just in relationship to their own myopic, immediate needs.

All organizations operate within much larger ecosystems of organizations and people. These ecosystems are like pointillist paintings, composed of many people and organizations, that require the viewer to take one, two, three steps backwards to see the whole picture. Within these free-flowing spaces, ideas, people, and resources follow the path of least resistance, which may be led by an organization — or, more often in Big Small Towns, catalyzed by individuals. As a result, organizations — and their leaders — need to learn to follow as much as lead. For instance, the Human Rights Coalition (HRC) wasn't interested in undoing "Don't Ask, Don't Tell" until a group of gay veterans forced them to pay attention to the issue and make it a priority. Following the passions and interests of their constituents, even if reluctantly at first, enabled HRC to tap into the passion of their constituents and row in the same direction toward a mutual goal. This is a much more fruitful path than trying to create a passion for a constituency; that most often ends up being both exhausting and unsuccessful.

The Importance of Being Known

For the first several centuries of our history, the lives of too many people, particularly women, minorities, children, low-income people, and people with unpopular opinions, were undervalued. They could be killed, ignored, overlooked, or marginalized without any recourse, because, to put it bluntly, they didn't matter enough to be fully protected societally. This began to change with the advent of television in the middle of the last century.

In 1965, Bull Connor turned fire hoses on peaceful protesters in the streets of Birmingham, AL. What would have been a local event before transfixed a horrified nation. The fact that the cameras were on at the same time as the fire hoses ensured that the victims of this assault, unlike the millions of African Americans abused in the Jim Crow South, were known. And so it went — when a television camera happened to be nearby, the rest of us could see and empathize with the previously unseen victims of racism. But, too often, cameras weren't around to capture the everyday slights and the egregious offenses.

On February 26, 2012, a young African-American man was shot to death in Florida. His death was ignored by the local police and press. But not everyone shrugged. Trayvon Martin's parents were not willing to let their son be an inexpensive byproduct of institutional racism. When the police refused to arrest George Zimmerman, their son's killer, they took their cause to the Internet, with millions of potential sympathetic allies. They used a petition on Change.org and encouraged bloggers and other influential people with large social media megaphones to tell their story until they finally got the nation's attention. They didn't need broadcast media to be heard, although they eventually found their way to it. At no other time in history would we have known about Trayvon Martin's death. Trayvon's parents insisted on it and ensured that his life and death mattered. If someone had taken a video on their cell phone of the incident, the world would have paid attention much sooner. There is no more "local" news — everything that happens is shared and experienced together instantly.

As mentioned in the previous chapter, social media enable us to choose to be known to more people. This is called being "onymous," the opposite of "anonymous." Being known more means stepping out into the world with our own identity, taking ownership of our opinions, and sharing what we like and dislike with others. The cumulative effect of being known is enabling others to have a fuller understanding of a person and all of the things that make her unique, interesting, and passionate. Being known in Big Small Towns creates a powerful sense of Matterness that is in direct contrast to feeling anonymous, unimportant, and overlooked. Using social media in Big Small Towns, we don't need to have a position or be famous to be heard or have influence.

In the spaces in which we are known online, civility prevails more often, and, when we choose to be known, we can matter more, individually and collectively. Choosing to be known makes it more likely that a person can be heard rather than dismissed as a troll or crank. Being known is contagious and makes it more likely that other people will choose to be known and express their views as well. Being known is a crucial building block for civil interaction and one of the most important gifts of living in a free society.

Big Small Towns in Action

Like many newly married couples, Michael Wood-Lewis and his wife Valerie began thinking about where they wanted to raise their children in the late 1990s. They wanted a small community, one filled with neighborliness, where people were friendly, took care of one another, and were engaged in the schools and town affairs. If one didn't mind the long winters, Burlington, VT, seemed the perfect fit, and, in 1998, they moved there.

Their first summer, living in a townhouse in the Five Sisters neighborhood, Michael and Valerie returned from a day out to find their neighbors packing up grills in the middle of the street.

Michael went up to a griller and asked, "What was this?"

"It was a block party," the man answered.

"But we live on the block. How come we didn't know about it?" Michael asked.

"Well, you will. It'll take about ten years, and then you'll just know."

Michael and Valerie were frustrated that they weren't getting to know their neighbors more. Valerie decided to do something about it and baked cookies for the neighbors. Rather than put them on paper plates, as Michael's mother used to do in Indiana, she put them on dinner plates, the best way to ensure a return visit, she told Michael. Their neighbors were delighted to receive the treats; however, the plates didn't come back.

People were moving in and out of Burlington, VT, as quickly as they were in Sleepy Hollow and every other part of the country, leaving neighbors in physical proximity to one another without any real personal or emotional connections. In addition, the changing economy made having two or three jobs to make ends meet the norm, significantly reducing the time people have during the day to bump into one another. Michael and Valerie wanted more from their community and felt instinctively that the mutual concern for one another and the sharing of resources and news, the fuel for sidewalk conversations, were all there just lying fallow, waiting for easier pathways to develop. In 2001, they began an email list for neighbors to share questions and concerns. There was one simple rule: No personal attacks. Attack the problem, Michael likes to say, not the person.

People began to share. *My cat is lost. I need a babysitter Saturday night. Why isn't the town fixing the sidewalk? Has anyone found my keys? My store is having a sale on jewelry this week.* By 2006, Michael decided to make a full-time go of his email list by turning it into a website called the Front Porch Forum. The Forum organizes conversations by neighborhoods of up to about 1,000 residents.

Michael Wood-Lewis instinctively understood that the fewer strangers there were in his neighborhood, the more likely people are to share information and help one another. Michael created Front Porch Forum to turn his new hometown, Burlington, VT, from a collection of strangers into a community of neighbors.

We met on the sidewalk in front of his house in July 2013. Michael doesn't fit the stereotypical image of a neighborhood organizer, with his pressed khakis and a blue, button-down short-sleeved shirt with a pen neatly tucked into his shirt pocket where a pocket protector should have rested. He was trained as an engineer and has an MBA, but his life's work turned into something quite different from those rigid endeavors.

Walking through the Five Sisters neighborhood in Burlington, VT, with Michael was a study in keen observation. He noticed new cracks in the sidewalk and a small headstone dedicated to a recently passed opossum resting against the side of an elm tree on the grass near the street. That elderly man just hired some high school kids to pick apples from his tree while he's away on vacation, he says, and that family over there just hired a new babysitter. Michael isn't a gossip; he is sharing information that has been posted on Front Porch Forum.

Running the Forum is a hands-on endeavor, with moderators choosing what they consider the most important postings and putting them at the top of the listing every day. Comments are screened for civility. Some of this activity has become automated; when a person posts too many times, it triggers an automated email suggesting that we all take turns to be heard (oh, that this could be implemented also at in-person meetings!).

Elected officials use the Forum to share agendas for upcoming meetings. Business owners share news and concerns. Posters can share ideas that they saw online from other towns ("We should try this recycling program they have in Yakima"). Some of the conversations can get heated. A post about a burglar spotted in a neighborhood that described him as a black teen triggered a two-week discussion on the appropriateness of using race in the description.

The conversations on the Forum change by neighborhood. In rural areas, the listings tend to be about pigs on the loose and bear sightings. In the Old North End, a low-income, blue-collar neighborhood, listings are largely about drugs and crime. The Forum isn't a newspaper; it is a series of conversations that would have happened on local sidewalks or in coffee shops before we were all so busy during the day. The expectation is that someone will post information and others will respond in agreement or disagreement, with additional information, or with an offer to help.

There are 16,000 households in Burlington. Front Porch Forum has more than 13,000 Burlington users (some households have more than one account). Neither age, income, nor neighborhood has been a barrier for participation. Overall, the site has 54,000 users in Vermont. In the summer of 2013, the site expanded to the entire New England region.

I met several of Michael's neighbors and Forum users literally on his front-porch. None of them were native Vermonters. When they moved to Burlington, they all heard from local people that the best way to learn about what was happening was to join the Forum. Giselle, who moved to Burlington to attend the University of Vermont, said, "I lived in Boulder, CO, for three months, and it was really tough to meet people and find furniture. I don't want to live like that."

What makes the Forum work? I asked Heather. She said, "It's a different experience from Facebook, where people are talking about themselves and posting pictures. It's not creepy, like Craigslist can be. It's not filled with spam. My Facebook friends are from other times in my life — college and high school. Front Porch Forum is right here and now."

Users also mentioned the importance of people being known to one another by using their first and last names and their street name (although not their house number) as identifiers. This helps to reduce anonymous sniping. Being known online translates into being known on the street after a post ("Did you find someone to tend your garden when you're away?"). Stuart Comstock-Gay, a member of the Forum in his tiny town of New Haven, VT, had a kiddie pool stolen from his backyard. He posted the news on the Forum. "It wasn't important from a cost perspective," he said. "It was just for the dogs to cool off in, but I wanted to post it on the Forum so that it was known to the community that this happened."

What's the big deal about a site with listings about sidewalk cracks and car break-ins? Every conversation on the Forum builds Matterness between neighbors that, in turn, generates more trust between them. Trust turns into reciprocity on small issues like returning a set of lost keys, which then transforms into collective action around big issues, like a proposed condo development one block over. Michael said, "You start with lost cats, and then you end up with, 'Let's go to the planning board meeting.'"

Front Porch Forum and similar efforts serve as platforms and infrastructure that scale Matterness in communities by making it easier to participate and be heard in neighborhoods.

Front Porch Forum starts in physical neighborhoods and expands online. Jennifer James's Big Small Town starts online and extends on land.

Jennifer's first daughter was born in 1998. Three years later, she had another girl. She loved doing all of the "mom" things she had looked forward to doing, but she was also lonelier than she expected. She wanted to talk to other moms and share experiences and ask questions. The easiest way for her to do it in 2001 was to hop online from her home in Winston-Salem, NC, and start blogging. She loved it, and she was very good at using her blog to connect with and talk to other moms. How long did you breastfeed? Is your daughter walking yet? When should I start to look for a preschool? There was an entire community of moms who shared her concerns and had answers to her questions. Jennifer looked forward to sharing her days and her children's milestones and progress with her blog community.

After a few years of blogging, though, it became clear to Jennifer that she was never going to be a big-name blogger, someone with a huge following with advertising dollars and a salary to match. She is a private person and is loath to share intimate details of her life, a requirement of online celebrity. But she loved talking to mom bloggers; it made her feel like she was part of a smart club. That's exactly what we need, she thought, a mom bloggers club, a place online for mom bloggers to gather and talk about their work and generate business opportunities together. She posted on her blog about the idea, sent out emails to her blogging friends, and got an instant and overwhelming response. Jennifer started the Mom Bloggers Club in 2007.

Mom bloggers have to be approved to join the club, but there are no fees for members, and membership in the club grew very quickly. At first, this was a passion project for Jennifer, even though it took a lot of time to organize and manage the site and the conversations. Then consumer brands began to notice how many moms she was reaching through the site. Her club members are the influential consumers, with big megaphones, that consumer brands like Advil and Bounce are no longer reaching through broadcast media. Jennifer was reluctant to monetize the site at first but then realized that she could accomplish many things by connecting with consumer brands. She could make a living running the Club, plus, she could connect her members to brands who would pay them to write sponsored content for them. The Club now has more than 19,000 members, 15,000 discussions, and 500 groups for moms to plug into a wide variety of topics to discuss, and it is a win/win/win for Jennifer, her mom bloggers, and the brands.

And yet, for Jennifer, something was still missing. "How can we help other moms around the world with our megaphone?" Jennifer wondered. Again, she asked her community if anyone was interested in joining a new site called Mom Bloggers for Social Good. On this site, nonprofits and corporations sponsor campaigns for the bloggers to join and, in some cases, sponsor trips overseas for them in order to help spread the word about efforts to alleviate a disease or hunger or poverty.

Jennifer Barbour blogs under the name "Another Jennifer" — and, no, not every blogger on these sites is named Jennifer. She joined the Social Good site because she wanted to put more meaning into her work. She said of Jennifer James, "She always sends you stuff, action steps, here's how you can get involved, here's why it matters to moms. Important information on maternal health, stuff that we care about and can click and tweet. It's a very easy way to be involved with social good in general, a nice introduction to topics and ways I can have a voice."

Jennifer Barbour went on a one-week trip to Nicaragua, sponsored by Water Aid America as an observer. In one of her posts during her trip, she wrote, "I've been amazed at the high level of poverty and near absence of running water all around me. I found out that less than 20% of people in this area have access to basic water and sanitation. We have seen some taps in the urban area of Bilwi that are connected to the municipal supply that are completely dry. I'm told they get water only every two or three days."

UNICEF reached out to the mom bloggers regarding a Newborn Action Plan to increase the health of newborn babies in impoverished countries. They didn't just ask the moms to spread the word about the report, they asked them to weigh in on it. Jennifer James said, "They really wanted to hear from regular moms about this important initiative. Our voices really are making a difference." The scale that Jennifer has reached with her blogs dwarfs anything she could have done in an analog age.

Jennifer James created a Big Small Town of people, organizations, resources, and needs that expands around the world. Her skills as a curator of information, trusted negotiator, facilitator of conversations and listener are critical to the success of her efforts. Her communities of mom entrepreneurs are trying to create some sustainability out of the assets available to them — their experiences, wit, empathy, storytelling abilities, and the social media tools at their fingertips. Jennifer connects them to one another and to consumer brands in engagements of mutual interest. She conducts the orchestra of her ecosystem with an eye for what is in the best interests of her network, which sometimes means taking a pass on an offer to work with a brand her network of moms doesn't like. And how does she know what her moms don't like? Because she is in *constant conversation* with them, asking them questions, getting their input, making sure that they matter most in this joint endeavor. As we will see in subsequent chapters, Jennifer's approach of being in *constant conversation* with her constituents ensures that she is working *with* her bloggers and never *at* them.

Core Components of Big Small Towns

Big Small Towns have a common set of characteristics in how they are structured and operate. These characteristics include:

Social Spackling. Spackling is a kind of putty that seamlessly fills cracks in walls. With a few layers of spackle and a little sanding and painting, there is no evidence that a crack ever existed. Our communities needed a new kind of glue, social spackling, to fill in the gaps left by the disruptions of the last few decades. Social spackling makes Matterness move around between people and between people and organizations. Spackling includes digital tools, platforms, and sites that form connections between people, allow strangers to meet or long-ago friends to re-meet, and creates community intelligence. Social spackling enables disparate groups to become a constituency with a common purpose, whether that purpose is cat loving or coding or Tea Party politics or vampire slaying.

Local intelligence used to exist because people lived in one place their whole lives and knew whom to count on, where to go for what services and goods, and the history of the people who lived in the community. Now, in our fast changing communities, everyone has access to social spackling tools that enable people to find the other peas in their pod. Social spackling sites include Yelp and Angie's List that create local intelligence for services, restaurants, and businesses. And don't forget *Meetup.com*, local blogs that are filling in for local newspapers, keeping residents advised of school and city developments. Facebook groups and sites like Front Porch Forum enable neighborhood residents to share news and help one another.

Dating sites are the ultimate social spackling. It can be difficult to meet a romantic partner locally when everyone is moving around the country so quickly. Dating sites like *Match.com* have become the new infrastructure for matchmaking. A Pew Research Center survey in 2014 found that 59% of adults thought of online dating as a good way to meet people, up from 44% of adults in 2005.

In 2010, the John L. and James S. Knight Foundation decided to conduct an experiment with social spackling by underwriting a game they called "Macon Money." Here is how the game worked;

Ruth Sykes is a lifelong Macon, GA, resident. Well, nearly lifelong, if you discount time away for college and just a few years after college. Without any prompting from me, Ruth described Macon as a "really big small town." There are lots of new people moving in, she continued, but it is likely that you will know someone walking down the street. There are about 100,000 people living in Macon, but there are lots of people coming and going because of several local colleges, including Mercy University, Middle George State College, and Robins Air Force Base. As Ruth says, "I feel like we do see new people coming and going — as educators and as medical professionals."

Ruth heard about "Macon Money" through a friend who was hired to help manage the effort. The goal of the game was to introduce Maconers to one another. Each participant received half of a bond, and their charge was to find people holding the other half. The winners received coupons redeemable at dozens of local stores. Participants could search for their partners either online through Facebook or a Meetup, or on land at an event at a local store. Ruth was excited to join the game, but friends of hers were skeptical. "I had some friends who were very nervous. 'What if I meet Jack the Ripper?' they asked. I told them to be responsible. Meet at a public place, like a coffee shop, where you could come and get your Macon Money bond. Or you could match with someone at the Meetup or at the Macon Money office downtown."

Ruth enjoyed playing the game. "It was nice to have this virtual cash that you could go spend and check out new places. I tried a lot of new restaurants. All the new restaurants I tried are now regulars in our family. I went to little boutiques downtown I had never gone to. "Macon Money" was such a conversation starter. I shopped and ate my way through Macon!" One of her matches was a man opening new loft spaces downtown across from her office. Upon further conversation, it turned out that the man's mother was a neighbor of Ruth's. She continues to see him once or twice a month when he visits his mother.

A year after the game ended, Ruth reflected on its impact on Macon, "It's good that we have the technology and the opportunity to do these things. If doing these things virtually results in a face-to-face relationship, that becomes one more human experience that you share, and that is great!"

Once people come together because of one shared interest in a game like "Macon Money" or a Meetup of Siamese cat owners, it is likely that there are additional areas of mutual interest. Maybe someone else has a daughter interested in botany school, and another bird watcher had a breast-cancer scare last year. *Can someone recommend a good car mechanic for Ed, whose car died in his driveway this morning? Mary lost her job as a receptionist at a dentist's office — anyone know of any jobs for her? And where's Dave? He said he'd be here. Can someone check on him to make sure he's OK?*

Social spackling helps local people come together, but what happens when we travel to new communities? Our networks travel with us.

Traveling Online Networks. Our analog networks were land locked and stationary. Our digital ones are expansive and mobile. The difference between our old, on-land networks and our new online ones is the difference between exchanging a business card and connecting on LinkedIn.

Exchange business cards with Joe Smith at a conference, and it is likely that those cards have an average shelf life of two years or until one or both of you changes jobs. You are likely to send that person an email in 2½ years and have it bounce back as undeliverable.

Connect with Joe Smith today on LinkedIn, or any other online network, and you will continue to be connected to him when he moves to his next job, and his next city, and the job after that. The connection is with Joe the person, not Joe the job. According to Adam M. Grant, the author of *Give and Take*, "The vast majority of the time, we fall out of touch by accident — we've moved, changed jobs, or just become busy.... This is one of the virtues of LinkedIn: It's easier than ever to track them down and reconnect."

The fact that our networks easily travel with us through space, time, and employment means that our ability to influence the people in our networks increases exponentially as the people we know stay with us longer. Not only do online networks enable people to stay in contact longer with one another as they move physically and through employment, online networks enable us to stay in contact with much larger portions of our social networks longer than ever before.

Social networks are simple structures that consist of nodes, people, or organizations, connected to one another through ties, or relationships. In 1973, Mark S. Granovetter defined these ties as "a combination of the amount of time, the emotional intensity, the intimacy (mutual confiding), and the reciprocal services which characterize the tie." On one end of the continuum are the strongest ties in one's life, immediate family, say, and at the other end, weak ties, such as people we just met and acquaintances. We spend most of our life interacting with and thinking about our strong ties; however, it is the weaker ones that kick our Big Small Towns into high gear by significantly expanding our social circles. Again, social media didn't create weaker ties — they make it easier to maintain and activate ties, particularly weaker ones, and take them with us wherever we go.

Without weak ties, we would all be cocooned in our tight cliques. Research on Facebook has found that these weak ties enable us to bump into new people on the site rather than just sitting with our seven closest friends in a vacuum-sealed echo chamber. One study about Facebook and this phenomenon stated, "It is our diverse collection of weak ties that most powerfully determines what information we're exposed to."

In addition to weak ties, there is yet another set of ties written in invisible ink on our network maps: Dormant ties or the people we used to know. Dormant ties include a colleague from a job eight years ago with whom you lost touch after you both left that company. A former boyfriend or college roommate with whom you haven't talked in ages are also dormant ties. Over time, many of these relationships fade, like the color in old photographs.

The reason dormant ties are so important is that they connect us to different sets of people and ideas and experiences. A study from MIT shows that ideas, career advice, and connections from dormant ties are even more valuable than those from current ties. Social media make it possible to find and re-activate these long lost people.

Big Small Towns are dependent on all of our ties — strong, weak and dormant — to infuse them with ideas, people, expertise, and resources that aren't available through on-land connections only. These ties are the critical resource that make Big Small Towns infinitely expandable.

A Low Threshold for Participation. Living in Big Small Towns creates opportunities for participation in a variety of interesting ways across income, position, and race. Broadening the network of people who participate in community life increases the likelihood that Matterness becomes more important in their interactions. Once people exercise their right to speak, they begin to insist on being heard.

For instance, a local planning board can use a Facebook group to engage the community in a conversation about a proposed condominium development on the site of the old canning factory. Public officials could use the group to share information, ask for input on the site — not just at the meetings — and correct misinformation.

Social media are asynchronistic, meaning they allow people to participate when they're free, at midnight, at six a.m., not just when a meeting is scheduled at Town Hall at seven p.m., which may be bath and bedtime in your house. Participation in a wide variety of events and activities is now possible for people who may not have the position or the time to participate in traditional ways. But participation is not limited only by time and position — it is also constrained by personality.

In her book *Quiet*, Susan Cain writes about the many ways quiet people participate online that would be very difficult for them to do on land. "...Introverts are more likely than extroverts to express intimate facts about themselves online that their friends and family would be surprised to read..." In addition, "The same person who would never raise his hand in a lecture hall of two hundred people might blog to two thousand, or two million, without thinking twice."

And quiet people aren't just participants online — they're leaders. I facilitated a group discussion for the Case Foundation with leading online organizers for causes. All but one of the nine participants described him or herself as an introvert. These were fantastically successful organizers for some of the largest causes in the country, including The Humane Society, the American Red Cross, and National Wildlife Defense Fund. But almost every one of them said they would rather read a book than go to a cocktail party. Social media provide them with opportunities to share information, connect people to one another, and organize events without having to endure the painful rituals of public participation. Quieter voices and people can be heard now in ways never before possible.

Physical limitations are a huge problem for millions of people. According to the Census Bureau's data from 2010, 56.7 million Americans are living with physical disabilities, about 18.7% of the population. Four in ten disabled people in their prime working years of 21-69 years old are employed, compared to 80% of adults without disabilities.

Social media provide amazing opportunities for people with a variety of physical limitations to manage their own businesses, in their own way and time. Barbara Wilson is a self-employed trainer/facilitator and guide-dog owner from County Tyrone in Northern Ireland. She is visually impaired and an avid Twitter user, accessing it with software that turns the text messages into voice messages. She said, "I tend to tweet things which might make other non-disabled people think. If I was out with the dog and there was a car on the pavement, I'd write that I had to walk on the main road, which everyone understands is very dangerous when you can't see." According to Disabled World, "When you do not find the accommodations you need among employers — make your own."

Innovation Ping Pong. Twenty years ago, magazines like *Governing* and the *Harvard Business Review* were the primary hubs for sharing information about innovative ideas. All you needed was a subscription to the magazine and a few months to wait for articles to be written and arrive in your mailbox.

Today the Internet is awash with ideas that get posted, downloaded, tried and refined in the space of days and months, not years. Ideas are generated through contests like the X Prize for innovative space travel and smaller, but still important, conversations about, say, local business shopping days. Great ideas, or just so-so ideas, or even the kernel of an idea can get refined, tested, and shared at Internet speed. These real-time laboratories of experimentation act like enormous games of ping-pong.

Here is how it works.

Alan posts about the success his community has been having in Battle Creek, MI, reducing the use of plastic shopping bags. *Ping.* Sam sees the post and says they tried something similar in Denver last year but with this additional component. *Pong.* Sally prints out the conversation and takes it to her meeting with the *Keep Seattle Clean!* task force. *Ping.* And on and on, ideas fly back and forth, online and on land and side-to-side. Never in the history of the world have ideas moved faster from inception to testing to refinement. Innovation Ping Pong is also an area within Big Small Towns where people are playing multiple roles.

Anyone can be an idea generator, refiner, tester, or sharer at any moment in time, without permission or restrictions. In addition to sharing ideas, online networks are filled with smart people willing to share their expertise with people directly. "Hey, Steve, would you mind Skyping into a meeting of our neighborhood group to give us some advice on the town's proposed zoning changes?" "Hey, Virginia, would your friend Mary be willing to speak to my daughter's class about jobs of the future?" Our social connectivity and the easy spread of ideas can help communities on a small scale, while expanding individual influence on a large one.

Mattering More in Big Small Towns

Living in Big Small Towns enables individuals to matter more in their lives and the lives of other people around them. We are sharing ideas and getting input on them from our crowds, participating on land at a town hall meeting and sharing the results online, or organizing an auction to help a family who lost their house to a fire.

This is only a start, as we become more influential we can also become more intentional about how we are participating in our communities.

Here are a few ways we can matter more in our Big Small Towns.

Own Your Social Media. Have you ever given up on your dinner companion who is more interested in checking emails and responding to texts on his phone than in your conversation? Have you seen kids who are more interested in preserving their high jinx with their friends on video than just enjoying the moment?

Almost ninety percent of Americans own a cell phone. Young people send an *average* of 110 texts per day. The ease of use of social media, coupled with the fear of falling behind and the exuberance of users, has created an avalanche of messages and images that is nearly impossible to absorb and manage on a daily basis.

Being at the mercy of our gadgets has created a sense of helplessness. I cannot turn off my gadgets for fear that I will be even more overwhelmed by messages requiring immediate attention when I turn them on again. Social media are the toddler asking endless "Why?" questions, insisting on our immediate attention. Our gadgets insist on our attention right now. *Pay attention to me! Answer me right now! Read these three blog posts and your tweet stream, and did you see that amazing photo on Facebook?* It is a dizzying array of requests and expectations that cannot possibly be sustained by most people. Choices need to be made about when, where, and how we are going to live online. We need to do a better job of filtering out the noise and shutting down regularly to re-energize ourselves. But we also can't forget that we are just beginning to understand this new way of living and that it will take some time to figure out how to make sure we don't lose ourselves to our devices.

Arnold Samlan was determined to reclaim his online social space. He shared a new set of rules that included: Adding humor and joy to his social media postings and inviting others to do the same, taking down the curtain by sharing personal information online, and exercising ownership over his channels. His social media are his to use as he sees fit, and others need to follow his rules or go elsewhere.

We should all follow Samlan's lead and mark out our own expectations and rules for engaging online. Perhaps you want to shut down on Sundays or reduce the number of social media platforms you are on. Maybe you want to make Twitter for professional use and Instagram for personal use. Maybe you want to blog less often. Now is the time to figure out exactly what you want from your social media channels, what you can contribute to them, and how to structure their use and your life to make it an energizing, rather than draining, experience.

Take a Chance. People need to participate in the ecosystem in order for Big Small Towns to work well. We cannot lose the power of serendipity now that we are sliding into patterns of using social media. Everyone can and should step out into someplace new and meet someone new and do something interesting. This was the point of the "Macon Money" game, but we don't need a game to begin.

Try one new thing — a new hobby, a local committee, comment on a blog, post a photo on Instagram or SnapChat. Find your passion, but don't just take from the Web — contribute to it. Play a different role than you usually play: Organize a Meetup rather than just attend one, or ask a question of your ecosystem online rather than just make a statement. Play, share, invent, curate, celebrate — give more than you take from your Big Small Town.

Renew Dormant Ties. Latent ties in your network are waiting to be renewed and re-energized. Make a plan to reach out to a few people a month whom you haven't connected with in a while. Not in the, "Here are all the great things I'm doing now," email-blast way, but in a personal way. Ask how they are, and what you can do to help them, and offer to make connections for them that might be useful. Since your ties are with you for the rest of your life, anything you give to your network will come back to help you in the future.

Conclusion

In the small towns of our collective, sentimental memories, the ones like Sleepy Hollow, residents felt connected to one another, had a sense of belonging, shared resources, pitched in when needed, and made lifelong friendships. *Mattered* more to one another and to the town as a whole. These weren't convenient attributes or desires; they were and are fundamental needs of human beings.

Big Small Towns are filling these same desires today. Regardless of the city or state we are living in, whether it is new or old, whether it began online or on land, on the coasts or in the middle, Big Small Towns enable us to do what we have always done well: Share local news and come together with people online. People are creating local connections that used to be generated by bridge club or through church, but ones that aren't bound by agendas, bylaws, boards, annual dues, committees, or fundraisers. We are free to just meet other people, express our innate socialness and desire to be neighborly and meet people with similar interests and hobbies outside the structures and rules of organizations.

Discussion Questions

- What are my Big Small Towns, and how do I participate in them?
- Are my online and on-land communities robust enough for me to know what is going on around me and to be energized through my passions and interests?
- Am I intentionally thinking of ways to engage less-obvious people, such as quiet people, in my efforts?
- What efforts am I making to stay connected to my weak and dormant ties?
- Am I reaching out online to unusual people and places for fresh ideas?

MANAGING MATTERNESS

Working From the Inside Out

INDIVIDUALS ARE ENERGIZED and empowered within Big Small Towns. Unfortunately, too many organizations, afraid of the world and the uncontrollable people who populate it, continue to work in walled-off ways *at* rather than *with* their own constituents.

Leaders who see the world as frightening, filled with threats and competitors, create organizations that are fear-based. This is a choice, not a necessity. We can choose to wall ourselves off, self-absorbed and unwilling to work together to build a better society, which is the antithesis of Matterness. Or we can choose to see a world of abundance and unlock our doors and appreciate the fact that people are naturally and overwhelmingly kind and generous and want to be helpful. Living and working through an abundance lens enables us to recapture the fundamental humanness that makes us empathetic, kind, and creative, and provides a foundation for building an equitable and just society.

This chapter will explore why organizations are stuck in their fear-based cultures and the resulting centripetal force that keeps them inside what I call "The Churn."

Fear-Based Organizations

The Citizens United decision by the Supreme Court in 2010 reaffirmed the court's hard-to-swallow definition of corporations as people. However, there is an advantage to thinking about organizations this way, which is to assume that they have the same flaws and limitations of people. They have mid-life crises (New Coke), they have hissy fits when things don't go their way (music companies suing teenage downloaders), and they can have terrible antennae for suitable marriage partners (Time Warner and AOL). And they are often paralyzed by fear and criticism.

Fear-based organizations are risk averse and wildly sensitive to criticism, whether it is real or not, legitimate or not. In these kinds of environments, staffers aren't trusted to make decisions, and constituents are stored in little, inflexible categories with no free will, while organizations largely go it alone, without availing themselves of the smart people sitting all around them waiting to be asked to participate in meaningful ways. These kinds of environments are bureaucracy's best friends — slow, suspicious, and suffocating.

We Care About Our Customers! Our Community Sustains Us! We Value Your Opinion! These blithe mantras are tacked to the walls of organizations everywhere, and, while many managers think their organizations actually mean them, the reality is that there is a huge disconnect between the interests of organizations and the needs of their customers. Not only is the gap huge, the unwillingness of organizations to even acknowledge the gap is often unshakable. This fear and distrust of what exists outside their walls makes it impossible for many organizations to step confidently into the world and create and deliver products and services *with* people rather than *at* them. It is enormously draining for a person, much less an entire system, to be on permanent high alert for attacks.

Fearful organizations spend enormous amounts of time in meetings strategizing about what to do to protect themselves from the world. How can we control the use of our content and make sure no one steals any of our good ideas? How can we stop staff from going off the cliff on social media and keep our reputation intact? How can we protect ourselves from wingnuts and whackadoodles intent on destroying us? The only way to make sure none of these things ever happens is never to do anything.

This approach was possible, if still draining, in the past, when the only outlet for an unhappy customer was a letter to the owner of a company or a long harangue to be endured by a small circle of people. But now every person is holding a giant megaphone that can expose the bad behavior of organizations — or reward good behavior.

Fear-based organizations tend to respond to criticism by blaming the critics. This often turns out to be a poor decision, especially if the original goal was to try to contain the criticism. For example, the United States Tennis Association (USTA) sued the makers of a documentary film about Serena and Venus Williams in 2013. Technically, the suit was about the use of twenty minutes of footage without permission. Untechnically, the suit was an attempt to quash the documentary because it showed Serena Williams' outburst at a lines judge during the 2009 US Open. The outburst happened on live television. Fans saw it, news broadcasts showed it, and bloggers and reporters wrote about it. But the USTA was still embarrassed by the incident and felt that trying to stop the documentary would erase the incident from our consciousness (although the slew of videos on YouTube replaying and satirizing the outburst will never allow that to happen). The effect of the lawsuit was to turn an obscure and innocuous film into a sensation. The filmmakers, I hope, sent the USTA flowers and candy.

Anything bad *could* happen; however, nothing bad is *likely* to happen. Fearful organizations confuse the possibility of something going wrong with the probability that it will. It is far more probable that no one will care about your organization than that it will be attacked. To continue to operate under the expectation of disaster is a problem of perspective. These organizations, and the people inside of them, see the world from the inside out, which automatically puts the needs of the organization ahead of those they serve.

Working From the Inside Out

People within organizations are often as confounded as people on the outside as to why they are being misunderstood or ignored. Here is an exercise to begin to understand inside-out organizations. Put a large piece of paper on a table, and draw a big circle in the middle of it. Inside the circle, write all the great things your organization does. *We feed the hungry. We manufacture quality hardware for furniture companies. We help people rehabilitate from serious injuries.* Without touching the paper, stand up and walk around to the other side of the table, and look at what you wrote. Unless you have special optical skills, it isn't easy to read what's written inside the circle. It wasn't written for you. That's what people outside an organization generally see when trying to figure out what an organization does. They may have a vague idea of what you are trying to do, but it's all a bit fuzzy and isn't meant for them. The focus on internal issues and needs rather than on Matterness, combined with jargony insider language, results in keeping outsiders, well, outside.

A study by IBM's Institute for Business Value outlined the perceived reasons for creating a social presence for businesses versus the perceived needs by customers. What it found clearly illustrates how far apart they are in their interests:

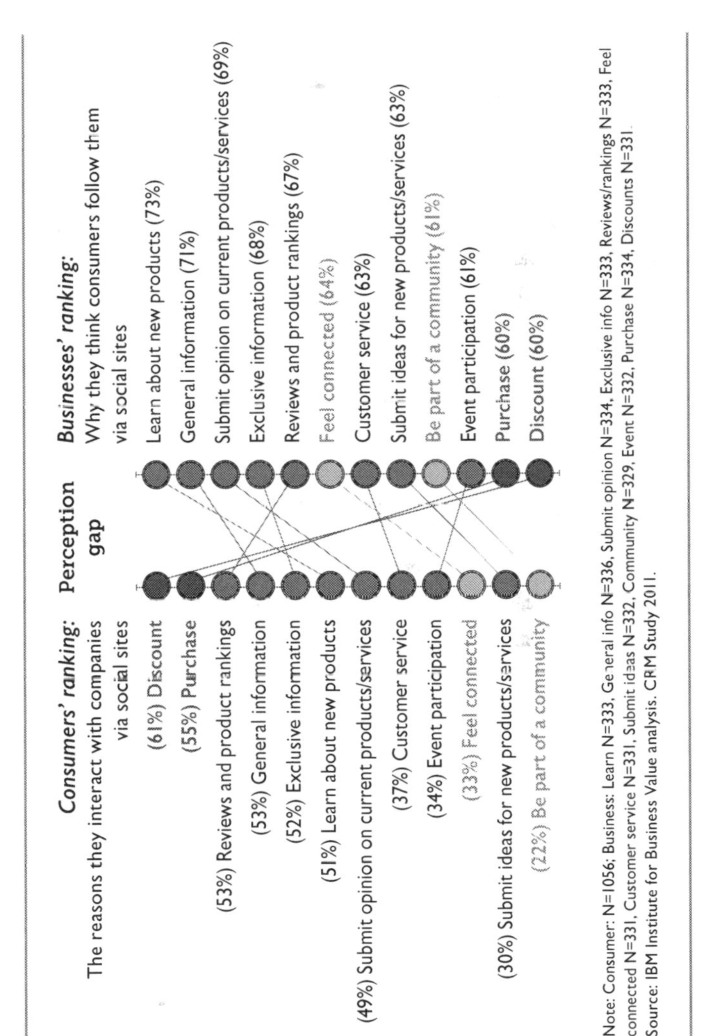

Clearly, there is an enormous disconnect between the kinds of things people want (discounts) and what organizations want them to want (learn about new products.) As described in *Made to Stick*, the sociologist Elizabeth Newton captured the distance between what organizations think they're doing and what people experience in a game called "tappers" and "listeners." Tappers were asked to tap out familiar tunes using their fingers on a table, and listeners tried to guess the songs. The tappers assumed that the listeners would get the songs they were playing 50% of the time, when, in reality, the listeners guessed right just 2.5% of the time. The reason is that the tappers were hearing the songs in their own heads, and, of course, the listeners weren't. Organizations are the tappers, assuming that who they are and what they do is as crystal clear to the world as it is to them.

Examples of organizations working from the inside out abound. Have you ever made a call to schedule a doctor's appointment and spent the first ten minutes giving them your insurance and billing information? What can be more distressing than having the people who should care about your physical health as much as you do demonstrate that they care more about your insurance instead? My heart goes out to the people charged with managing the paperwork in these offices, but the press for their paperwork clearly overwhelms the interest they have in you as a person or a patient. Of course, doctors' offices are overwhelmed with insurance and financial contretemps, but they have allowed it to overwhelm the experience of patients as well. When was the last time you were thanked by a doctor's office for choosing them as your provider over the myriad other choices you have?

Museums work from the inside out when, after spending extraordinary amounts of time curating exhibits, they do a terrible job explaining to visitors why these particular works of art were chosen. Yes, I could rent the audiotape, but I have already paid to see the exhibit and should able to understand why, exactly, this particular work of art was chosen for this exhibit. When a curator chooses not to tell me why these particular pieces of art were selected for this exhibit, what they are really telling me is that I don't matter. An exhibit like this may meet or even exceed projected output measures (*Hundreds of people visited our exhibit in October!*) but will fail the Matterness test by leaving visitors feeling unappreciated and irrelevant.

Surely this is not the intention of the doctor's office, nor is the museum trying to alienate attendees. Unfortunately, as an overwhelming amount of research show, most organizations don't really want to know that customers are confused or unhappy. Research shows that organizations routinely ignore complaints and even constructive suggestions. "Many organizations still regard customer complaints as not only an unpleasant fact of business life but also as a waste of time and money in investigating these concerns." This is in the face of research that shows clearly that "...organizations that encourage customers to complain are very successful."

This research proves the power of Matterness because just the ability to complain and be heard — and not feel ignored or dismissed — makes a person feel better. The problem doesn't even have to be fixed for the complainer to feel valued by and better about the organization. Unfortunately, most organizations hide behind a velvet curtain because most people don't complain — they just leave.

Even when organizations walk through the motions of getting feedback, the ubiquitous customer-satisfaction surveys often miss the mark by overemphasizing *their* process over *your* experience. *Were we friendly to you?*

Were we on time? Did we fix the problem? Do you like our widget? Would you recommend us to a friend? We really want to know how we're doing! That's difficult to believe because research shows that, "even organizations that solicit feedback rarely listen to it." Not every complaint or suggestion needs to be acted upon, but every single one deserves a listen.

Organizations are as defensive as the people that work for them. It can be painful to hear people complain about one's work; it can also be dangerous to one's ongoing employment to pass it along internally. Most staffers who hear complaints don't pass them along internally — they blame it on the complainer.

Organizations treat even well-meaning critics as nosy mothers-in-law: Annoying, judgmental, critical nags who range on a continuum from distractions to annoyances to destructive forces. All too often, organizations assume that complainers and whackadoodles are the same thing. Of course, there *are* whackadoodles out there, and they should be avoided, but there aren't nearly as many as most people assume. The fear of whackadoodles is allowed to take up an enormous amount of space within organizations, which is an enormous shame. It is like allowing the class bully to keep you from playing on the playground.

Critics often have a legitimate beef. The fried calamari *was* cold. The front desk clerk *was* rude. This store needs to carry tall sizes, too. This feedback — which is *free* market research — is more often ignored than accepted. These critics generally get a cold shoulder or a brittle, defensive response written in a lawyerly tone: "We find no evidence at this present time of the aforementioned unpleasantness mentioned on this weblog." Or the limp "Thank you for bringing this to our attention. We will look into the matter." A matterless waste of words. Or, if something really big blows up, then the apology team rushes out with, "We are so sorry if our words were taken out of context and may have offended someone." We have already seen how powerfully painful the absence of Matterness feels to people, and these kinds of responses trigger those feelings of powerlessness and unimportance.

Organizations are remarkably adept at assuming that critics are aiming their complaints at someone else. I once sat in a room full of executives from large family foundations. We were listening to a conference call with a consultant who had been hired to survey grantees of foundations from around the country about their interactions with these foundations. The results were a predictable litany of complaints that boiled down to the foundations being aloof and unresponsive. In the middle of the call, the CEO of one of the largest foundations in the country pressed "mute" and asked the group, "Did they survey any of our grantees?" The participants shook their heads, "No." "Well, then," he said, "this clearly has nothing to do with us."

The consequences of working this way, from the inside out, divorced from the real concerns of constituents, are enormous. At the most obvious level is losing customers. The cost of attracting a new customer is five times that of retaining an old one. Just by increasing customer retention by 5%, a service provider can increase profits nearly 25%. Clearly, keeping existing customers is critically important for the long-term success of any organization. And, of course, the opposite is also true: A consequence of working divorced from the world becomes an inability to attract new ones.

The idea that customers are unhappy and feel unheard isn't new. Expensive consultants are telling organizations this every day. Shelves of business books implore businesses to treat customers better, to engage in conversations with them, and to become customer-centric. And yet, organizations continue to operate in the same inside-out ways. Why?

Because of The Churn.

The Churn

All organizations need to get stuff done. They need to manufacture things and sell them, serve people, advocate for legislation, and change the world. The puzzle to be solved internally becomes: "What are the most efficient and least-risky ways to use the fewest resources to generate the biggest bang for the buck?" And in that answer, "The Churn" is born — the obsession with internal processes at the expense of relationships.

The Churn is the centripetal force that pulls organizations inwards, making them far more concerned with crossing off their to-do lists, completing transactions, and avoiding risks than with understanding and appreciating their constituents. The Churn is so loud and insistent that it drowns out the concerns and interests of constituents. The people inside an organization may want to listen and help, but, too often, The Churn makes it very difficult to do so. Within The Churn, immediate production and transactions outweigh everything else, particularly Matterness.

This comes into sharp focus when meeting agendas are created. The Churn, powered by the gnawing fear of anything possibly going wrong, creates mind-numbing staff meetings stuffed with planning and process issues: *Who is on call this weekend? When is the new inventory set to arrive? How many families did we treat last week? What are we going to do about the cash flow/revenue shortfall/unexpected-legal-expenses problem?* Even if all of these data are already available within the organization's management systems, staff and organizers feel compelled to talk about it, because the shadow of The Churn extends over everything these organizations do, like a menacing rain cloud.

The Churn creates endless conversations about what could go wrong, what might go wrong, what will go wrong unless we keep talking about our fear of something going wrong. It is the foundation for the micromanagement of staff by managers terrified of staffers doing something wrong — or even something different. The Churn and all of the fear and risk aversion inherent in it turns little mistakes into huge problems, like typos on a blog post or a joke on Twitter that someone finds offensive. Events that either aren't worth worrying about or could be fixed by a simple, heartfelt apology become the fodder for even *more* meetings and discussions.

The Churn is not the result of a particular type of managerial style. It is the overriding culture of risk-averse organizations obsessed with efficiency and overwhelmed by the demands of always-on technology — meaning it is the culture of most organizations.

Inside the vortex of The Churn, work becomes a dispiriting grind. A survey of more than 12,000 workers found that most of them had no time for creativity at work (70%), no time to focus on just one thing (66%), and no opportunities to do what they enjoy (60%). All of this happens in the face of overwhelming data that says that energized, creative, independent, and refreshed workers create successful companies — actually cause these companies to be successful. In short, according to experts, "Put simply, the way people feel at work profoundly influences how they perform."

The Churn creates cultures that insist on treating constituents less like human beings and more like commodities and data points. Constituents are batched, coded, and categorized. You are a direct-mail donor, or an online buyer, or an empty nester, or a Republican primary voter, all neatly stored in large databases and managed by algorithms. Constituents become just one small part of the Great Big Churn of paperwork, sales, tickets, and donations. Each one of us, inside and outside of organizations, is Charlie Chaplin turning with the gears inside the enormous machinery created to ensure that someone else's quarterly budget projections are met.

In a study of intermediary organizations whose fundamental purpose is to connect organizations to one another, Rich Harwood wrote, "What is noteworthy is that, despite their impulses and aspirations to undertake and sustain engagement, these organizations and leaders find themselves enveloped in a profound and airtight gestalt of inwardness, planning, and professionalism."

Most organizations assume that The Churn is the inevitable price of doing business. This passivity is not only counterproductive, but it can even be downright dangerous. On December 1, 2013, a Metro-North train traveling south in the Bronx went flying off of the tracks, killing four people and injuring more than seventy. The findings of the investigative report into the accident read, in part, "The findings of Operation Deep Dive demonstrate that Metro-North has emphasized on-time performance to the detriment of safe operations and adequate maintenance of its infrastructure." The Churn won out over common sense and customer safety.

The Churn creates the pressure to focus on transactions with constituents. *Close the sale, get the check, fill the seats!* These transactions become far more important than building relationships and understanding the interests and needs of constituents — unless they relate to closing the sale and getting the check. The Churn is in charge when organizations treat 500 customers whom they should know like 50,000 generic ones, using impersonal email tools like Constant Contact. This is why we get emails that purportedly come from the CEO of the company but are actually just from a fake email address (info@acme.com). This is why organizations use conversational platforms like Facebook primarily to tell us how great they are, how many widgets they sold, and how much money they raised. They use the greatest conversational media in the history of the world to show off and pose as peacocks rather than learn from constituents.

As we'll see in the next few chapters, leaders need to make a conscious choice to undo or avoid The Churn. This is important not only for organizational success but for personal success and sanity as well.

The New Now

Our always-on culture has us furiously multi-tasking every minute of the day. "I can do lots of things at once," say my multi-tasking companions, tweeting and Facebooking simultaneously. Actually, you can't. Once our attention is divided, it is the same as having none at all for most people. Short bursts of complete attention are preferable to long periods of constant interruption.

People need their full attention to live and work well. Many studies have demonstrated the inability of people to function optimally while multi-tasking. Distracted driving, even hands-free cell phone use, has become more prevalent and just as dangerous as drunk driving. One finding was that "...heavy media multi-taskers are distracted by the multiple streams of media they are consuming, or, alternatively, [that] those who infrequently multi-task are more effective at volitionally allocating their attention in the face of distractions." In other words, multi-taskers are in a constant state of distraction, getting nothing of much value done. This is the New Now.

Put all of these multi-taskers together inside of organizations, and, presto! we have extraordinarily distracted and inefficient organizations. From a study of these multi-tasking organizations comes this damning finding: “When managers multi-task, even small decisions can take days; instead of spending, say, a quality 15 minutes with people, they can only afford a rushed and ineffective two to three minutes.” Multiply this whirling madness of inefficiency by the number of managers in an organization, and a frantic, exhausting work life comes into focus.

When the internal culture is such that everyone is expected to respond to all messages the moment they’re received, organizations force staffers to breathlessly sprint through regular work hours playing a game of whack-a-mole. Then the “real work” gets done after hours, replacing playing with the kids or taking a yoga class or reading a novel. This is an exhausting and unproductive way to work. Busyness replaces thoughtfulness as the driver within churning organizations.

One terrible result of being constantly interrupted is the inability to distinguish among what is important, what is routine, and what is trivial. It is clear that some people need better guidelines as to when it is acceptable to be interrupted. Here are the instances that require immediate attention — worth disrupting a meeting or a meal or a conversation:

- Someone needs real medical attention, like stitches or an x-ray.
- Your house is on fire.
- Your biggest client just chose another company.

- Your mother is calling. (This is particularly true for my children!)

This is a list of real immediacies that can't wait. Everything else can wait at least an hour for your full attention — as it did for centuries without anything bad happening.

There are only a few professions that require constant attention deficit during the day: Political campaigns, news organizations, and emergency medical personnel. Everyone else just thinks they do, but, as your mother might say, "If everyone is looking at their phones and stepping into a manhole, should you?"

In addition to promoting frantic busyness, The Churn is also a driver of artificiality as a substitute for real and imperfect life.

The Desultory Effect of Fakeness

Organizations that are trapped inside their own organizations have too often fallen through the looking glass of no longer understanding what is real in their interactions with their constituents and what is fake. The more we *talk* about reality and authenticity, the less real and authentic we become. Reality is like silly putty when you play with it too long: It ends up being less flexible, a bit dirty, and not very appealing. Authenticity and the *appearance* of authenticity are different things that are too often confused. As Alice Marwick wrote, "Because self-presentation online is often tightly constrained, the normative impetus to be honest and truthful results in a *performance of authenticity*."

The line between real and fake, spontaneous and staged, heartfelt and cynical has become difficult to parse. Needing to parse them creates an even greater sense of cynicism. It is difficult to believe almost anything you see or read when the likelihood is that the event was staged.

Organizations that *don't* manipulate their constituents become incredibly valuable in their ecosystems. This is what makes Jennifer James and her platforms so valuable to her mom bloggers and what makes Front Porch Forum so different from a newspaper.

A common mistake organizations make is assuming that working in real and personal ways will take more time and energy than continuing to work from within The Churn. It isn't true. It doesn't take more time to treat people like human beings; it takes a different kind of commitment to the work. For instance, sitting down with ten season-ticket holders in a living room to discuss what people want to see, how much they can afford, and what it would take to recruit their friends is different from continuing to churn through ad buys that no longer work or email surveys that few people will fill out.

The Churn pushes leaders to outsource these conversations to staff or consultants. The point within The Churn is to just get the work done. However, it is critically important that organizational leaders participate in these kinds of conversations personally, to feel the energy of the room, and understand what matters to participants. This is why successful school principals walk the hallways of their schools and restaurateurs talk to their diners. Engaging directly with constituents starts to turn them from passive consumers into active problem solvers, as we will see in later chapters.

Conclusion

Fear-based organizations are on constant alert for threats and intruders. As such, they are burdened with internal cultures that are incapable of trusting employees to use their good judgments. They cannot easily and openly engage with their own constituents in the outside world, which makes them unable to listen to real complaints or engage in real problem solving with their supporters. Within these cultures, The Churn wins out. Rather than use social media channels for real conversations, most organizations use them as extensions of their old billboards and press releases.

Discussion Questions

- When has an organization made you feel like you don't matter?
- When has *your* organization made others feel like they don't matter? (You will actually have to talk to your constituents to learn the answer to this question.)
- What drives work inside your organization — efficiency or effectiveness?
- What measures are you using for success, and how are they driving The Churn?
- Are you making time and space inside your organization for thinking about what matters most to your constituents?

4

Leading From the Outside In

IN HIS ACCEPTANCE OF THE Nobel Peace Prize in 1964, Dr. Martin Luther King, Jr., said, "I refuse to accept the idea that man is mere flotsam and jetsam in the river of life, unable to influence the unfolding events which surround him." We should all join him in refusing this idea. We are all capable of action; moreover, we are capable of leading other people into action.

Leadership has always, and will always, be critically important to the success of any endeavor, whether it is a small team inside a large organization, a loose network of people, an after-school club or a spontaneous neighborhood effort. Appreciating and growing Matterness is the new competitive edge for organizations; it is the key to understanding that success isn't serving a lot of people but making those they do serve feel that they matter. This will create the ultimate goal for all organizations — repeat customers, long-term donors, and reliable volunteers. The spread of Matterness internally and externally makes leadership a much-easier and less-lonely endeavor by generating and spreading more energy, goodwill and capital around. This requires organizations — and the people who lead them — to switch from inside-out thinking to outside-in leadership.

This chapter outlines three crucial steps for a new way of thinking about and practicing leadership. It starts by moving from a scarcity lens to one of abundance, continues with a discussion of the need for leaders to recapture their humanity and become more vulnerable, and concludes with a discussion of organizations being in conversation *with*, not *at*, constituents.

Flipping the Lens From Fear to Abundance

As discussed in the last chapter, bureaucratic, micromanaging cultures, are, by definition, based on fear and distrust. Within these cultures, planners desperately try to ensure that nothing ever goes wrong, that every possible contingency has been answered. This is an impossible and exhausting way to work. Leading fear-based organizations is a difficult, lonely, uphill way of working because they are largely closed to the outside world. There is an alternative to a scarcity approach to the world, and that is using a lens of abundance.

Looking at the world through a lens of abundance enables organizations to recognize and connect with the large numbers of staff people and constituents who want to help. Abundance thinking creates organizational cultures that allow staffers to step out safely and smartly into the world. In addition, social media spreads abundance thinking by enabling organizations to quickly and inexpensively reach out into their ecosystems for assistance. This is more than optimism; it is a smart way of looking at the world and engaging with it.

Magical things happen in environments filled with abundance thinking. Jimmy Wales and Larry Sanger looked at the world in 2001 and saw a friendly place filled with smart, energetic people of goodwill who were willing to devote thousands of hours of free labor to create Wikipedia. There would be no Wikipedia, no archive of video of human-rights abuses around the world stored on Witness.org, no Political Ad Sleuths sponsored by the Sunlight Foundation to figure out who is underwriting political ads, without abundance thinkers leading the way. Abundance thinkers see a world overflowing with friendly people who are prepared to help in myriad ways and who are just waiting to be asked to do meaningful things to help. This is a fundamental tenet of Matterness — the powerful combination of the resources and goals of organizations with the skills and interests of constituents.

It is important for leaders to take a courageous look at their own organizations to determine whether — willingly or not — they are leading a fear-based organization or one tilted toward abundance. Here are a few questions for discussion to begin to understand whether an organizational culture leans toward scarcity or abundance:

- Do we spend more time in meetings discussing what could go right or discussing what could go wrong?

- Do we have lawyers on speed dial ready to sue any encroachments on our efforts? Are we looking for ways to try to control what other people do or ways to tap into their own natural style and creativity?

- Are critics treated as enemies intending to harm us or as friends who want us to do better?

- Do we trust staff to make decisions on their own, or do we feel we need to double-check and preapprove everyone's work, including messages on social media channels like Twitter?

These are not Yes/No questions, but the beginning of conversations about the assumptions that are baked into an organization's culture and processes. Here is a conversation I had with an organization about their fear of using Twitter. I asked the questions and they answered.

Question: Do we trust staff to post on Twitter without approval?

Answer: No.

Question: Why not?

Answer: Because a staffer may post something inappropriate.

Question: Like what?

Answer: Like using profanity we aren't comfortable with.

Question: And why might they do that?

Answer: Because they are young and inexperienced.

Question: What happens as a result of needing to review everyone's Twitter posts?

Answer: Our tweets take two days to get posted.

Question: Is that a good use of Twitter?

Answer: No.

Question: So, what could happen that would make it possible for young, inexperienced people to post smart messages on Twitter?

Answer: We could train them on what we expect them to post.

Question: And?

Answer: And we could correct them if something goes wrong.

Question: And?

Answer: And we could provide information at our Monday-morning meetings on topics to post for the week.

Organizations must challenge their scarcity assumptions in order to fully engage with constituents and understand how to make them matter more.

Local governmental agencies may be a surprising place to find abundance thinking, and yet, a growing number of them have been working with Code for America, organizing volunteers to code for municipalities across the country to turn government information into useful online applications. The idea of working with outside hackers without months of vetting would have been unthinkable for most municipalities just a few years ago. The success of Code for America is based on the openness of local governments to work with volunteer coders. The willingness of dozens of cities across the country to work with Code for America volunteers is not only a recognition that these volunteers have skills not often found within city or county governments, but also an understanding that code has become a key component of the infrastructure of civil society that increases Matterness between citizens and government agencies.

These partnerships can turn into extraordinary examples of abundance, like the one in the winter of 2012. That winter, the northeastern section of the country experienced a virulent outbreak of the flu. There were shortages of flu vaccines everywhere. People were calling doctors' offices and pharmacies with no luck. "Try again next week," they'd say. In October, a hacker in Chicago named Tom Kompare attended a conference in that city on the opportunities for open-source applications to support local government there. He decided to take a stab at a mapping application to indicate the location of flu shots with driving directions. Said Kompare, "In two days, I put up a proof of concept." Within a week, he was meeting with the Chicago Department of Public Health to refine the project. The City of Chicago integrated the app with their website, making information about available flu vaccines quickly and widely known.

Two months later, Mayor Menino in Boston declared a public health emergency because of the flu. Harlan Weber, the Boston captain for Code for America, remembered Kompare's efforts in Chicago. Boston coders repurposed the Chicago app in a day and had it posted on the Boston city website in time for a campaign promoting vaccinations in 24 locations. Thousands of people used the app to locate available flu shots.

These coding efforts cost the cities of Chicago and Boston nothing. The feeling of pride and accomplishment on the part of coders was enormous, and the benefit to the citizens of both cities, as the ad slogan goes, was priceless.

Ultimately, sustaining an abundance culture isn't possible without remaking the role of leaders, who, in turn, can remake the role of their staffs and, finally, their constituents.

Rehumanizing Leaders

Leadership doesn't happen behind closed doors, in a world marinating in social media — it happens in public. In order to lead effectively, one has to have the courage to step out into the world and engage in uncontrolled and unpredictable conversations with real people. This means choosing to reveal one's true self, including one's flaws and vulnerabilities, something most of us spend our adult lives trying to avoid. Being vulnerable in public is as appealing for most people as public speaking and wardrobe malfunctions. We want the world to see us as confident, happy, smart, got-it-all-together people, but leadership in ecosystems filled with other people and organizations is predicated on being more human, which means being more vulnerable. Only by understanding our own limits — our tender spots that make us feel less confident and more fearful — can we understand the vulnerabilities of other people.

The world needs to believe that real people work inside of organizations, because only real people on the inside are going to care about real people on the outside and ensure that they matter.

It isn't an easy shift to take off the protective armor we have been taught to wear in public, but we have to remember that we weren't born wearing buttoned-up shirts and blazers. We learned to protect ourselves from the real, imagined, and potential slings and arrows of the world. Now we have to re-learn how to do something more important: Connect in real, human ways with people inside and outside of our organizations.

Recognizing one's own vulnerability is a key leadership skill, not a detriment. When Henry Timms was appointed the interim Executive Director at the 92nd Street Y in Manhattan, the head of HR pulled him aside to give him advice. "Henry," he said, "You have just one problem. You know all the answers."

That's a problem? Henry wondered.

The HR director read his mind and continued, "It's a problem because it doesn't give anyone else a chance to weigh in and help shape solutions. You run things all by yourself, and that leaves everyone else out."

Henry had always considered being smart and having good solutions to problems an asset in his other positions. But opening himself up to the smarts in the room turned out to be a huge relief. He didn't *have* to have all of the answers; he just had to know how to elicit them from other people.

Staff people are supposed to have all the answers, we were taught. Showing uncertainty is a sign of weakness.

We need to reconcile these outdated notions of power with the new need to be the kind of person other people want to follow. Leadership isn't an office; it's a mindset and skillset that enables a person to knit together the mosaics of people inside and outside of organizations with all of their different skills and interests necessary to move an effort forward.

The following is a conversation I had with the CEO of a billion-dollar organization about his fears of revealing his true personality online.

"I can't be on Twitter," he said.

"Why?" I asked.

"Because someone is going to say, 'You suck,' and I'm going to lose my temper."

This is ordinarily a conversation stopper in C-suites and boardrooms. If there is a potential problem on the horizon, one that could cause embarrassment or, worse, a loss of control, the brakes are put on, regardless of whether it is likely that the bad thing will occur. This is the possible outweighing the probable. It is critically important for leaders to push past their fears and continue playing out the scenario. Here is how the CEO and I continued our conversation.

"Go on," I said to the CEO. "What happens when someone says, 'You suck'?"

"I'll Twitter that they suck."

"OK — what happens then?"

Again, this was brand-new territory for this CEO to think about.

"Well, I guess my communications people would make me apologize."

"And do you think you could do that?"

"Sure," he said, "I could say something like, 'I'm sorry I lost my temper, but I care deeply about my organization, and it cuts me deeply to hear someone unfairly criticize us.'"

"And then what happens?"

His communications chief took this opportunity to jump into the conversation and yelled, "And then the world would know what a great guy you are and love us even more!"

The fear of letting the world see him as a real person, temper and all, was stopping this CEO from thinking beyond his initial discomfort. His communications staff knew, though, that the only way to really step out into the world and become more connected to constituents is to be a real human being, messy bits and all. This assumes, of course, that one really wants to connect with constituents.

In the winter of 2014, Roger Goodell, commissioner of the National Football League, decided to host a Twitter chat. Chances are Goodell and his staff assumed he would have a short, friendly public conversation with football fans. And he did. There were a number of pleasant exchanges, but, because the conversation was on Twitter and organized by the hashtag #AskCommish, haters and wise guys could also post their thoughts and questions. Here is a tweet from Michael Curry, whose Twitter name is @mcurryfelidae07: "Who's more immoral? An employer that covers up his workers getting brain trauma or an employer tolerating abusers but not gays?" The NFL quickly and predictably declared success — and hasn't scheduled another Twitter chat since.

Many senior executives would have considered this exchange an uncomfortable public embarrassment and vow never to do a Twitter chat again. That's fear-based thinking that insists that an unexpected criticism is automatically an embarrassment. That kind of thinking assumes that these sentiments wouldn't exist if the NFL didn't create a Twitter chat to air them. An abundance thinker would have seen the Twitter chat as an opportunity to really talk to football fans about their concerns.

Goodell and his staff could have invited a few of the critics to his office or a restaurant to have a conversation about what they're upset about. And they could have all reported back on Twitter on how the conversation went, what they learned from each other, what they are still frustrated about, and how they may continue to be in conversation with one another in the future. This would have enabled the rest of the crowd, the football fans who may have *thought* what the critics *said*, to see that Goodell and the NFL aren't afraid of criticism and want to hear from fans on how to improve.

Critics need to be listened to because they want organizations to do better; otherwise they wouldn't bother criticizing. Nothing diffuses the anger of a critic more than being asked to expand on their concern. Engaging in conversation with them is the best way not only to defuse their concern but to show others that you aren't hiding from a real back-and-forth conversation. Converted critics often become a person's or organization's greatest fans.

Leaders can begin to rehumanize themselves by revealing themselves to their own staffs. David Bley is the Director of the Pacific Northwest Initiative for the Bill and Melinda Gates Foundation. His team is responsible for grant-making in the Pacific Northwest, dedicated to reducing family and child poverty, family homelessness, and to improving early-childhood education.

This is emotionally taxing, often gut-wrenching work for David and his team. It requires a personal commitment to improving the lives of the most vulnerable citizens, while holding onto one's own faith and humanity. David was faced with two challenges. First, he knew that a person's experiences and orientation toward the world shapes their approach to community problem solving, and he needed to know more about his staff's worldviews. In addition, "When you work in increasingly large and complex organizations, it can often be difficult to stay in touch with what your underlying aspirations are."

David is well aware that storytelling workshops have become cliché in many organizations, the stuff of staff eye rolling. Nonetheless, he decided to engage his staff in a retreat to tell their own, personal stories to understand each other better. This meant that David also had to fully participate and show sides of himself he doesn't ordinarily reveal during the course of a workday.

During the session, Bley and his team learned about a remarkable personal journey of one of their own colleagues. The staffer was the child of Cambodian immigrants who survived the killing fields. He was raised in a low-income family and won a Gates Millennial scholarship, becoming the first person in his family to go to college and then graduate school. Working at the Gates Foundation was a full-circle journey for this man.

Two-thirds of the stories shared by the team were new to others in the room, and this included many stories that David didn't know, and he had worked at the foundation for six years at that point. It created the understanding and connections that are helping the team tackle the most difficult social problems. David said, "We have a greater faith that we're going to figure this out together."

Participating in this kind of activity, Bley says, is Management 201, not Management 101. Making the time and space for learning more about each other and what matters to them runs counter to the process and workflow orientation of most institutions — in other words, it's the Anti-Churn. Managers have to personally participate in humanizing processes like these, to be models for staffs for managing unpredictable and uncontrollable territory. According to Bley, devices like the storytelling session open up the group to their own humanity and stop them from drowning in tasks and issues that aren't the most important things.

Rehumanizing Staffs

The rehumanization of leaders quickly bleeds into the culture of organizations, providing both the permission and opportunity for staffers to regain control over their professional and personal lives. Increasing Matterness internally means enabling staff to become decision makers and creative problem solvers. One way that staff can begin to regain control is to better control the technology that they feel is taking over every minute of their day.

When people say that technology is taking over their lives, they usually mean "email." *Ping, ping, ping*— every minute of the day, one's inbox is filling up with an endless series of memos (and spam) that puts us on call permanently. Not only is there simply too much of it flying around, but nearly 70% of what does fly around is spam or useless. Fear-based organizations use email as a liability tracker — a record of who said what, who decided what, who did what, in order to potentially be able to point fingers in the future. This creates a daily barrage of unnecessary communications, the reflexive reaction by staff to send everything to everyone.

There needs to be more intentionality built into internal communications that have too often simply slid into working quickly without thinking about the why. Organizations need to look at the communication needs of staff. Who needs what information from whom, and what are the best vehicles for doing that? A policy discussion should not be done by email. Links to interesting articles would best be done through an internal social network like Yammer. "Reply All" should, for the most part, be banned. Email is best to *confirm* things: A meeting time, a report completed, a site visit scheduled, follow-up activities from a meeting. Telephone calls and meetings are best for discussions (and, if they are well planned, they will take less time than a days-long email thread to complete).

Limiting the amount of time we spend on email requires more discipline than most individuals generally have, which is why leadership is important: It forces organizations to do the things that are hard but necessary. Leadership creates and reinforces cultures that help staffers stop playing their daily, never-ending effort of trying to keep up with The Churn that is exacerbated by email. Organizational leaders need to say, and exhibit, the rule that returning emails within twelve hours is their expectation — not within five minutes. Organizations' meetings need to begin by asking everyone not to put their phones on vibrate but to turn them off, or even put them in the middle of the table. It means encouraging employees to shut down for at least one weekend day.

Focusing on the well-being of employees, providing them with mental space and freedom to think and dream, is a fundamental part of undoing the always-on culture that feeds The Churn. In *Overwhelmed: Work, Love and Play When No One Has the Time,* author Brigid Schulte tells of the work changes at the Department of Defense spearheaded by Michele Flournoy, who was the Undersecretary of Defense for Policy in 2009. Flournoy instituted a flexible work program, in which employees were "held accountable for getting quality work done by certain deadlines. As part of this process, they were given more control over their schedule for when, how, and where they met those deadlines." Schulte writes, "If the Pentagon can do it, why can't you?"

Menlo is a software company that was created by its founders with one simple idea: Work should be joyous. It can be so only when workers control when and how they work. Menlo employees choose when they want to work, which is not 24/7, like most technology companies. In particular, the company insists that employees leave work behind at the office. As Rich Sheridan, the co-founder, said, "If you have time for your life, you are joyful. And when you come to work in the morning, you're more creative, more imaginative, and more excited to be here."

Menlo's success demonstrates that the use and control of our devices is a leadership choice. Menlo's approach runs counter to our deeply embedded Protestant work ethic. But those norms were created in an era when people had to stop working because the sun went down. We need to reset norms about when work is productive and when it is simply a meaningless, mind-numbing grind. Organizations need to be mindful of the physical and emotional toll of an always-on culture. Matterness for staffers involves choosing for themselves how they want to work, not being defined or dictated to by others.

Volkswagen stepped up to this challenge in 2011, when one of their manufacturing plants in Germany started a new policy (created as part of their union contract negotiations) to shut down email servers from 6:15 pm to 7 am. The 3,500 employees at the plant are delighted to regain their personal lives and time. Other German companies are beginning to replicate this policy. Profits at Volkswagen in general, and productivity at this plant in particular, have gone up significantly since the policy was instituted.

Being in Conversation With Constituents

The final step to rehumanizing organizations is changing the relationship between organizations and their constituents. This happens through conversations — lots and lots of conversations. Organizations must be in constant conversation with their constituents. *Ridiculous!* You may be thinking. *I am on conference calls all day long. I sit through slide presentations, board meetings, and staff meetings every day. I am on my cell phone from seven in the morning until I walk in the door at eight at night. I couldn't possibly be in one more conversation with one more person that is going to reveal anything I haven't heard.*

But these aren't conversations — these are the noisy part of The Churn. The Churn causes internal people to become mired in internal processes, discussions of internal processes, reviews of internal processes, and endless to-do lists that never get shorter. All of that internal pressure has a cost, and the cost is time *not* spent in conversation with customers, clients, and donors building trust and long-term relationships. Conversations with constituents are part of the Anti-Churn, the way to get out of the frantic, internal, do-everything-by-ourselves grind.

Conversations are real back-and-forth dialogues and entail real effort by both parties to understand the other. It requires listening on both sides and encouraging the people who care most about an initiative to weigh in on important issues. A conversation is something you have when you are interested in learning about the other person and how they think and feel. The Churn is when a person spends time trying to poke holes in the new idea from the head of marketing instead of saying, "go."

Real conversations often get confused with formal data-collection efforts using tools like surveys, focus groups, and interviews. However, leaders need to remember that formal data-collection efforts are entirely one-sided and devoid of Matterness for most constituents. It is relatively easy to make sure service people have more time between service calls or to provide a message saying how long the wait is for the next service operator or how we can mail out our product faster. It requires greater intentionality to listen to how and why customers could matter more to an organization.

Traditional organizational communications efforts have largely boiled down to paid, broadcast media like radio commercials and newspaper ads, and declarative statements on social media. Being in conversation is different. Conversations don't have to be long and involved; they don't have to include a life story or baby pictures. They have to be sincere and unscripted. The only way for organizations to be in conversation with constituents is for leaders to encourage unpredictable and uncontrollable conversations. Conversations will go where constituents want them to go, not necessarily where organizations want them to go — just ask Roger Goodell.

Social media have fundamentally upended traditional organizational communications because they are by nature multi-directional media. Organizations can use them to speak to the world — and the world can speak back. Organizations accustomed only to broadcasting messages can be taken aback when constituents insist on being listened to. The Susan G. Komen Foundation never expected that their Facebook page would become the center for complaints from people upset that they defunded Planned Parenthood in 2012. They shut down their Facebook page rather than talk to critics because they were not in the habit of being conversational. After a week of horrible publicity online and on mainstream media, Komen reversed their decision and funded Planned Parenthood. The imbroglio damaged their reputation and ultimately cost the organization millions of dollars in donations.

Real conversations between people and organizations are largely uncontrolled, but that does not mean that they are by definition leaderless. Leading conversations involves asking questions that organizers are sincerely interested in hearing answers to. Leaders keep conversations on track online and take them off line when necessary. And leaders are the ones who say, "We've heard a lot of great ideas — now let's try this one."

Conversations are uniquely powerful experiences for leaders to engage in and not outsource. Leaders must be involved in these conversations — not with everyone, perhaps, and not all day, but enough to connect in meaningful ways with constituents. Mrinal Desai, the co-founder and VP of CrossLoop, understands what it means to be in conversation with his constituents. He answers every email and comment made about the company. When he engages and discusses why something happens, often he changes someone's mind — and they become the company's greatest ambassadors.

Boris Groysberg and Michael Slind call this "Conversational Leadership." They wrote, "Smart leaders today...engage with employees in a way that resembles an ordinary person-to-person conversation more than it does a series of commands from on high. Furthermore, they initiate practices and foster cultural norms that instill a conversational sensibility throughout their organizations."

Groysberg and Slind limited their observations to leaders having conversations with staff, but there is an opportunity to extend conversations into the ecosystem. Anytime and anywhere opportunities exist to have regular conversations with people farther away from the core, they ought to be embraced.

EMC, a global conglomerate providing computing-support services like cloud storage, content management, and extra storage, seems like an unlikely organization to be at the forefront of encouraging staffers to be in conversation with their constituents. However, EMC encourages its employees to talk to the world about their work on their own blogs, even critically, because it is a great way to hear how employees and constituents are thinking about EMC. It also shows the world that the organization isn't afraid of frank conversations.

Jargon as a Barrier to Conversation

One enormous barrier to being in conversation with constituents is the use of organizational jargon that gets in the way of outside people understanding what inside people are talking about. An organization accustomed to regularly testing their language and communications with outside people would never post this Mission Statement:

> We are a fun place to work and play.
> We have a courteous and fair approach to relationships.
> We have a qualified and approachable staff.
> We're passionate about our community.
> **That's who we are.**

Presumably, someone on the outside would have pointed out to this group that it never mentions what the company actually *does* (in this case, it's a tennis center). However, in the same way that it is difficult to ask questions you don't want to hear the answers to, it is difficult to check whether the acronyms and language used internally every day to organize the work makes sense to anyone on the outside.

Social scientists invented a phrase, "natural language," to refer to the words regular people use and understand. It is defined by the *Oxford Dictionaries* as "A language that has developed naturally in use (as contrasted with an artificial language or computer code)." Perhaps it is a reflection of how far we have come from natural language that we need a phrase for it. Business people have created their own unnatural language by hijacking the English language. This is how we get words like "synergy" and "paradigm shift" and events like "town halls" that don't actually involve real conversations; it's how we are taught that photo ops and broadcast updates by email are perfectly acceptable substitutes for real conversations. These artificial words and events create barriers to hearing from constituents. It's difficult to return to regular human conversation from a career spent sticking to talking points — but it's not impossible.

Here are a few pointers for beginning real conversations with constituents (or for restarting them if your effort has stalled):

- **Guidelines need to be in place.** Every organization needs clear, written expectations for who is allowed to say what to whom. Hopefully, the guidelines will be expansive and encourage more people to speak on behalf of an organization than fewer. These can be social media guidelines, but most organizations find that the issues that are covered in social media guidelines are already largely addressed in their employee handbooks.

- **Give more than you take.** Which conversations in your life are more interesting: The ones with the people who tell you everything they've done and want you to pat them on the back? Or the ones with the people who want your input and advice? Be the person who listens to what other people have to say, not the one who goes on and on about how great you are.

- **Become advice seekers.** We're thinking of streamlining our offerings: Should we just offer X or Y? We usually have a dinner dance in the spring. Do you think we should do one this year, or do you have a better idea? Switch your communications from declarative statements to important, open questions.

- **Put a face on it.** No one likes having a conversation with a logo. Organizational accounts are fine and necessary (particularly when staff turnover is likely); however, it is still important to let constituents know with whom they are speaking. And don't be afraid to show your real personality in conversations. And literally put a face on it, put up photos of the people behind the work.

- **Let your staff go.** If you don't trust your best ambassadors, the ones who know the most about your efforts, the ones you spent hours interviewing, to talk about the work, then why did you hire them? AARP has clear guidelines in place and has hundreds of staffers on social media channels every day talking about their work. Staff are trusted and trained to speak with people. This is a key element in scaling Matterness that will be discussed in more detail in the next chapter.

- **Mistakes are inevitable.** Even if guidelines are in place, mistakes are going to happen. Every person and organization makes mistakes out loud using social media, and very rarely are they important ones. An abundance culture recognizes that mistakes happen and that the sky doesn't fall. Apologize, and move on.

Conclusion

Working hard and fast, having lots of messages and people vying for your attention doesn't change once The Churn is no longer in charge. But the actual work does. When time is no longer sucked up by hours of discussion of what could go wrong and how to retain control and how to convince people to like you and buy from you, then time can be spent in conversation, asking for input and advice, creating new collaborations with people and organizations. Perhaps for the first time, you can take advantage of the abundance of new capital floating around.

Discussion Questions

- When do you/your organization slide into scarcity thinking? Are there particular issues or concerns that trigger this kind of thinking? If so, when and why and how can you move toward abundance thinking?
- How do people inside and outside the organization view you as a person and a leader? (This is going to require courage to ask for and use this information.)
- With whom are we having conversations and about what? And are these real back-and-forth conversations or broadcasts of talking points?
- What happens when someone criticizes your efforts? Do you engage them in a conversation or ignore them and hope they go away?
- Who do we celebrate and why? Who else could we celebrate for their efforts on our behalf?
- Are we offering meaningful ways for people to help? Are we asking for real input on important issues? Are we learning together with our community?

SCALING MATTERNESS

5 Scaling Matterness Within Organizations

THE LANGUAGE OF STRATEGIC PLANS is embedded in organizational life. Words like "goals," "objectives," "strategies," and "tactics" have dominated organizational life and filled bookshelves for decades. This approach and lexicon served a purpose once to try to bring perfect clarity to work and organizations. Now, however, they have become a 1965 Cadillac: Big, pretty, very slow, and very expensive (but, boy, you should have seen the tail fins on that car!). The world is not waiting for anyone to craft a perfectly aligned five-year plan that will be outdated by the time it is implemented.

Organizations need to be organized around core operating principles rather than plans. This is the difference between trying to stick to an unchanging roadmap spread out on the passenger seat while driving sixty miles an hour and plugging a destination into the GPS that recalculates as you go. Simple, clear principles provide ongoing guidance and enable staffers to act in smart ways on behalf of organizations. Following principles assures organizational leaders that everyone associated with the organization has the same clear expectations of what is supposed to happen and why.

This chapter describes why and how core operating principles increase Matterness within organizations. This chapter closes with cautionary tales of the bad things that can happen when organizations stick to plans instead of principles.

The Purpose of Principles

Operating principles are not mission statements, vision statements, or goals. Principles are the fundamental rules by which an organization works. They provide the scaffolding for participants, staff, volunteers, and board members to work and make decisions based on the best interests of the organization. They don't need to be updated every six or twelve months. Plans are timed; principles are timeless. Plans change; principles don't.

Working by plans that become formulaic in a fast-paced world flies directly in the face of both the hopes and costs that go into hiring a single new manager. On average, the cost of hiring a management-level person, which includes time spent crafting the job description, posting the job, reviewing resumes from and interviewing multiple candidates, checking references, and hosting an in-person walk around the office comes to about $18,000. Add in the time for training, and the total cost for an organization to hire a new manager is upwards of $20,000.

Once hired, the first thing most organizations do is to tell these smart, responsible, self-starting, creative people not to think for themselves but to work according to the organization's tried-and-true formulas. Research shows that employees hired to work within cultures that value agility and creative problem solving stay longer. According to one study, "Users and team members of agile projects have consistently shown higher motivation and satisfaction compared with projects that use plan-driven methods."

Staffers need to be encouraged to make mistakes and learn from them. But this will happen only when leaders are working by principle and are not bound by counter-productive micromanagement.

Working by principles frees leaders from micromanagement and enables them to use their time in different and more productive ways. Leaders can worry less about the process of work — and watching workers work — and more about making work meaningful for staff. They can focus on building in restorative time and opportunities for creativity on a daily basis and through a career. Conversations with constituents become a primary concern, not an afterthought, and progress toward successfully incorporating principles becomes more important than tracking transactions. Leading this way ensures that Matterness will flourish.

The armed services of the United States and many other military forces around the world operate by a set of principles called "military doctrine." The purpose of the doctrine is to enable members of the different branches of the armed forces to work in concert under the same framework of language and ideas and to provide guidance for individual soldiers during the inevitable uncertainty of conflict. "Doctrine for the Armed Forces of the United States," published in 2013, is the latest statement of core principles by the Department of Defense. It states that the purpose of military doctrine is "providing fundamental principles that guide the employment of US military forces toward a common objective." Furthermore, "The use of joint doctrine standardizes terminology, training, relationships, responsibilities, and processes among all US forces to free joint force commanders (JFCs) and their staffs to focus their efforts on solving strategic, operational, and tactical problems."

Most of us are not, thankfully, going to war; nonetheless, the need for core principles is essential for all organizations in providing a fundamental set of common beliefs during the frenzy of day-to-day work.

Developing and Using Principles

Principles are simple statements. This sounds simple enough, and yet, when you look at mission statements, websites, and organizational literature, you find that they are overflowing with complexity that contribute to The Churn. In his book *Insanely Simple*, Ken Segall describes simplicity as the love child of two of the most powerful forces in business: Brains and Common Sense. It is easy to slide into organizational complexity because it reduces the need to make hard choices and risk offending someone by not including an option. Complexity is generated from the kind of groupthink that ensures that my clock radio has nineteen different settings — seventeen more than most anybody needs. Developing core principles makes it easier for everyone in an organization to both manage the work and contribute to its efforts.

It would be ironic, in the least, for me to suggest a set process or formula for developing principles. However, there are two recommendations for developing principles that organizations would be wise to heed. The first is that they should all be infused with Matterness. Core organizational principles operationalize the aspirational goals of Matterness and enable organizations to work in concert toward them. They ask and answer questions like: How are we going to ensure that our organization honors the people who work within and without? How are we going to ensure that we understand the needs and interests of our constituents well enough to serve them?

The second recommendation for developing principles is that they have at least the agreement, and hopefully the input, from the largest number of people inside and outside of the organization. It seems reasonable to offer the people who will be responsible for ensuring the use of the principles an opportunity to help shape them.

Principles don't state what doesn't need to be stated by organizations. For instance, it isn't necessary to state that every organization needs to be financially solvent to survive. And every organization needs to follow basic employment laws both out of basic decency and to avoid lawsuits. Core organizational principles are the foundation that is unique to an organization, just as the foundation to a house is unique to that building.

Here are a few examples of core principles:

- Hire good, smart people, and let them go.
- We defend employees from unwarranted attacks.
- Everyone matters.
- We work *with,* not *at,* people.
- Repeat customers sustain us.
- We are *great* at cleaning clothes.
- We value our clients as people as well as customers.

When an organization has a founder with a strong vision, principles may already be practiced but not necessarily written down. It is important to codify the principles by writing them down, sharing them widely, and reviewing them often, to ensure that constituents are continuing to honor and work by them. This is what Kip Tindell decided to do for his company.

In 1988, the Container Store was ten years old and growing rapidly. It had just opened a large store in Houston, and the resulting sales growth was astonishing. Most CEOs would be thrilled at that moment and do more of what they were doing, but Tindell, the Container Store's CEO, was concerned. *"How can we continue to communicate our fundamental values with the company getting so big?"* he wondered. He invited the entire staff over to the manager of the Houston store's home to talk about a set of foundational principles he had been thinking about for a while. Out of this conversation came the company's seven foundational principles that they still use today and have on their website. These principles include:

- 1 great person equals 3 good people.
- Communication IS Leadership.
- Fill the other guy's basket to the brim. Making money then becomes an easy proposition.
- The Best SELECTION, SERVICE & PRICE
- Intuition does not come to an unprepared mind. You need to train before it happens.

- Man in the Desert Selling.
- Air of Excitement.

The Container Store works hard every day to live up to these ideals. They find good, smart people (they hire only about 3% of applicants), train them well, and pay them 50–100% more than what other retailers pay their employees. Not surprisingly, their employees stay a long time. The company regularly places in the Top 100 Companies to Work For in *Fortune Magazine*. In addition, they work with vendors with a generosity of spirit (those are the people whose baskets are being filled.) And, of course, they make sure that customers matter the most — what they call “a genuine concern for customers’ needs.”

Using guiding principles can help organizations experiment with new projects that involve working in new and different ways with constituents. Two curators, Maria Nicanor and David van der Leer, at the Solomon R. Guggenheim Museum in New York City, were struck by the notion, that, by the year 2025, 75% of the world’s population will live in urban areas. What does this mean for how we will live and interact with one another? In collaboration with BMW, they created the BMW Guggenheim Lab Project to develop free public programming in three cities — New York, Berlin, and Mumbai.

The driving forces behind the Labs were the general interest in cities and how people live and interact in them as well as a general concern about urbanism. The project needed to escape the traditional methods of museum display in order to explore cities through an “out into the city” approach rather than discussing these topics indoors in a gallery setting.

The basic premise was for the museum to get outside of its walls and create opportunities for regular people, not just sophisticated museum-goers or policy makers, to think about and experience how cities of the future may look and feel. A clear set of principles was needed to hold all of the project elements together in one overarching rubric.

David and Maria had a strong vision of what they wanted to create in the Labs but decided to lead by principles and not plans. Citizen participation was critically important to their effort. They wanted each city's effort to reflect the unique style and cultural values of that place. They wanted their team to feel empowered to make decisions and help shape the project. Finally, they wanted to be agile and make course corrections as they went — not after the project was over.

Each city had its own unique combination of workshops, talks, activities (both online and on land), and discussions. In addition to planned events, there were also "pop up" or spontaneous events in the cities as well. The goal was for the museum to engage people where they lived and in topics of interest to their lives, not to create an artificial bricks-and-mortar exhibit for people to visit. In all, the project invited microbiologists, psychologists, architects, economists, television directors, athletes, engineers, photographers, medical-technology innovators, environmental-justice activists, journalists, tourism directors, tech geeks, yoga teachers, anthropologists, students, community groups, civic leaders, chefs, and florists to participate in the Lab programs.

In Mumbai, a city increasingly overwhelmed by people, the central topic that drove discussions and programming was privacy. In New York, the guiding theme was "confronting comfort," and gentrification became a hot topic. The Berlin Lab focused on "makers," a worldwide movement focused on ways to use, reuse, and recycle material to make "goods" that are valuable, creative, and relevant to society.

The New York and Berlin Labs both experienced anti-gentrification protests against the project. This was particularly true in Berlin, where a city-wide reaction to the BMW sponsorship raised questions about the intentions of the Lab prior to its opening. Intense media coverage spurred a parliamentary session led by the Mayor of Berlin about the goals of the project, a discussion that ultimately drove the direction of content for many of the Berlin Lab programs. Maria successfully testified in front of the Berlin parliament to defend the project.

Maria and David had full faith in their team. One of the team members, Elissa Edgerton Black, an Australian by birth and New Yorker by employment, wonders if the multi-national nature of the team itself required them to work by principles, since the work styles and cultural orientation of team members were so different from each other. Working by principle gave the staff freedom to chart their own paths while it also held them accountable to one another to stay true to the project principles. Working by principles gave the team the tools to "do" and "interact" in new ways and enabled the staff to successfully work in very different cultures in Berlin and Mumbai.

The BMW Guggenheim Lab continues to operate as a model for similar projects and urban-issues programs around the world. Its success can be boiled down to three critical elements: Understanding and articulating the core principles of the effort, recruiting strong team members who could both independently manage their areas and adapt their effort to the local culture and circumstances, and using data for real-time adjustments.

Moving From Defaults to Principles

As mentioned above, some organizations, generally those with strong founders, have principles that are embedded within the culture of their organization without necessarily being articulated. All organizations have embedded norms and expectations — these are their default settings, but, if left unexamined, they can become barriers to principles. These invisible default settings may not represent aspirational principles but the fear-based habits and assumptions of leaders. These assumptions need to be identified, challenged, and replaced by visible, widely shared principles.

The best way to begin this process is by using scenarios to practice putting principles into action. For instance, leadership may not realize that their defaults are set to distrust until they walk through a scenario of what they would do if critics posted on their Facebook page. Criticism doesn't have to become a crisis if the principle is that everyone — and what they think and feel — matters.

An organization could practice using the principle that we work *with* people, not *at* them. Scenario practice involves taking each core constituency and walking through exactly how the organization puts that principle into action. For instance, how exactly does the Acme Corporation work *with* rather than *at* its board when every meeting is largely a recitation of the financial statements, with no opportunity for input or discussion? Is information shared with members between meetings that provides a full understanding of what is going on? Does the creation of the board agenda involve the opportunity for board input? Are we giving board members ways to help the organization by engaging their own social networks to share information and get input?

Conversely, how is the Acme Corporation's board helping the staff to matter more? Does the board value the rate of transactions over the strength of the relationship between the company and long-time customers? Is the staff encouraged to creatively solve problems? Is the board forgiving of reasonable mistakes?

An arts organization may have inclusivity as a core principle, but how will it feel if a lot of non-members are coming to their programs and not giving donations? If they post our financials online during good years, will they do so when they are running a deficit? And will they engage in conversations online and on land with constituents about where we see ourselves going in the next few years, or will we simply post a final strategic plan, with no opportunity for real input?

Default settings are some of the most difficult organizational habits to change, largely because they are so often unspoken. The practice of identifying them through scenarios will not only bring them to light but also uncover additional assumptions and ideas that control organizational culture that staffers may not have felt empowered to bring up before. This kind of work requires courageous leaders, willing to challenge their own assumptions.

Once organizational principles are in place, some mechanism is needed to translate them into the day-to-day work of the organization. These are action plans.

Action Plans

Contrary to conventional wisdom, organizations don't need to create the best plans to be successful. Rather, they need to create the smartest plans for getting started that keep everyone connected to their principles and, by association, to Matterness. The greatest challenge in creating smart plans is keeping "analysis paralysis" at bay. The risk aversion that defines so many organizational cultures makes it nearly impossible to start something when there are unanswered questions. However, most questions can't be answered for a new effort — that's why it's new. Most existing efforts have unanswered questions about the future — that's why it's the future. Trying to collect data or answer questions that are not answerable is a poor use of time.

Smart action plans are those that have a realistic chance of working or, at least, enable leaders to learn about what could work. They include:

- Clear statement of principles.
- Activities for six to twelve months that answer the question: "Who is going to do what, exactly, by these deadlines?"
- Statement of resources. What exactly do we need in terms of people, expertise, code, inventory, awareness to be successful?
- Success questions. Defining the right questions to ask and answer throughout a six-month period is an opportunity to keep the focus on Matterness and not The Churn.

It is tempting to assume that revenue is the most important measure of success or failure for any endeavor. However, revenue is a product of action plans — not an input. The resources and activities that an action plan catalyzes will result in revenue (hopefully) and strong relationships within the ecosystem.

Every plan is infused with the exuberance of expected success embedded in it; however, success measures need to be balanced by failure triggers. Failure triggers are red flags that draw attention to a process that isn't working. Once an effort is underway, there will be lots of data, lots of input, and lots of conversations happening, and it can be very hard to know which ones to pay attention to in addition to the successes. Failure triggers provide assurance that the train won't be off the tracks for long without someone noticing. This isn't to assume that an effort won't be successful; it assumes that awareness and agility are necessary for making real-time course corrections.

A failure trigger could be that our team's season-ticket sales are more than 10% below last year's rate one month from the opening of the season. The trigger will lead to internal, and hopefully, external conversations. What could be the problems leading to this immediate outcome? They might include price, inflexibility of dates and times when tickets need to be used, an awful team on the field, or a bad in-game experience. Luckily for organizations, there are a whole array of social media channels to use to listen for failure triggers — but, of course, only if the organization is in conversation with constituents and listening.

Smart Data

Collecting and storing accurate and up-to-date tracking data are fundamental to any effort. It doesn't have to be a fancy or expensive system. It just has to ensure that, at any moment in time, key questions can be answered: Where are we in production? Where are our bottlenecks? How are expenses running against projections? What are our sales and donations now and against last year?

But a word of caution is needed: These data are critical to any effort; but because they are so transaction-focused, they are also Churn-bait. Organizations measure what they most value, and fear-based organizations most often value transactions over relationships. An additional set of data is needed to augment the transactional information, and these are smart data. Smart plans need smart data are order to be implemented successfully and provide information to inform real-time adjustments. Smart data focus on Matterness.

There was a time when data were very expensive to gather. It required surveys and interviews and focus groups, which often required outside expertise and time to complete. We are now swimming in a sea of digital data easily accumulated through clicks and hits, eyeballs and traffic. Aggregating enormous sets of data has become fashionable across sectors, but just because it's popular doesn't mean it's smart.

Big data is mainly useful in the narrowest ways. Amazon recommends books that are similar to ones I have bought in the past, assuming that I buy books only for myself and that my future interests perfectly match my past interests. These kinds of transactional efforts are interesting to people only as long as they fit their existing algorithms. The need for ad revenue drives the collection of big data. Search engines and online social networks developed "filter bubbles," a particularly insidious device for keeping our eyeballs focused on the things they want to sell us. The phrase was created by Eli Pariser to describe the ways that these companies are narrowing our search results and choices in order to better target ads. Pariser wrote, "More and more, your computer monitor is a kind of one-way mirror, reflecting your own interests while algorithmic observers watch what you click."

Big data and filter bubbles are the antithesis of Matterness. Matterness creates an organizational state of mind that encourages people to break out of their small silos and play multiple roles. It helps people create processes and products together and celebrates them for their humanity—not just their wallets. People are multifaceted, endlessly interesting, changing, and curious beings that cannot be captured by a sweep of data.

For the overwhelming number of organizations and efforts, smart data are far more important than big data. Smart data means collecting the least amount of information needed to answer the most important questions about Matterness.

Smart data focus on the experience and feelings of constituents, not primarily the internal processes of organizations. It takes careful and deliberate thought to ensure that questions of Matterness become the focal point of smart data collection. Online data can easily turn into vanity measures: Lots of people are clicking and sharing our information. But these data avoid the questions of "What and who matters to these constituents?" and, conversely, "What and who does the organization value?"

Again, one of the reasons to be in conversation with constituents is to ask for their help figuring out important issues like Matterness questions. Here are some sample Matterness questions:

- How do you feel when you think about our business/issue?

- Do you feel like you matter to us? Do we make you feel like a person or an ATM machine? Do we feel interested in us or in you?

- Do we remember who you are, or do you feel new every time you engage with us?
- Do we reach out to you only when we need something?
- Is it easy or hard to figure out whom to talk to about what? Do you have a sense of who our people are, what they do, and why they're here?
- Have we gone over the cliff of automation, where it no longer feels like human beings are running our effort?

Matterness questions extend beyond what happened to what didn't happen, meaning not just the existence of Matterness but its absence as well. Why didn't people come to our show? Why didn't donors give to this year's fundraising appeal? Why did we lose twenty regular customers this year? These are the data that organizations desperately need to find ways to connect with and tap into the energy of their constituents. Too often, we shy away from exploring the things that didn't happen because it feels embarrassing or shameful that no one showed up at last week's lecture or art show or sales event. This is when principles are the most important: To lift us up from disappointments and The Churn and help us remain aspirational in our efforts.

Cautionary Tales of Not Working by Principle

Organizations put themselves at risk of overreacting to threats when they focus more on plans than principles. Although every organization's principles will be unique to their particular interests and needs, one overriding issue for every organization is the need to protect their own people. Without that principle in place, there is no reason for anyone to work on behalf of the organization. How can anyone feel that they matter to an organization if they don't feel protected by them? Here are two stories of what happens when organizations are more interested in protecting their plans than their people.

Adria Richards was at yet another tech conference. A large part of her job was recruiting programmers for the small tech start-up she worked for, SendGrid. The company created an email-delivery service to help companies market their email messages and stay out of spam folders. At the conference, two men behind her were loudly making off-color jokes. Adria did what she does every day, she took a photo of them and called them out on their bad behavior on Twitter. The conference organizers saw the tweet and kicked the offenders out.

So far, the story is simple: Crude, sexist remarks were made that are contrary to the rules of behavior posted by the conference organizers, and the offenders are evicted. Then the story turned dark for everyone involved. One of the evicted men posted this message on Hacker News: "Adria has an audience and is a successful person of the media. Just check out her web page link in her Twitter account; her hard work and social activism speak for themselves. With that great power and reach comes responsibility. As a result of the picture she took, I was let go from my job today. Which sucks because I have 3 kids and I really liked that job."

The floodgates opened up, spewing hatefulness at Adria and SendGrid. She received death and rape threats on Twitter. The company's servers were attacked and had to shut down. In a panic to get their business back online, SendGrid fired Adria for complaining about the behavior publicly rather than privately. Then a boomerang backlash began as people who were livid that Adria was punished for asking for civility began to post messages outraged at SendGrid. The entire fiasco unfolded in less than a week. Reputations took a beating, jobs were lost, and a company was damaged, all because of a tweet calling out uncivil behavior.

On another coast, another employee was embattled in another tempest, but this time with her own organization. On June 19, 2013, Michal Kohane, an employee of the Jewish Federation of San Francisco, wrote a blog post on eJewish Philanthropy. She wrote, "I've had it with the constant song and dance around 'young adult engagement' as the only promise of any Jewish life anywhere ever at all.

Michal's post set off a firestorm of comments on the blog, some in support of her post, others opposed. Later that day, Michal was fired from her job, which created another backlash against the Federation. It was unrelated to the post, her boss said. The world did not believe her.

Both SendGrid and the Jewish Federation took bad situations and made them much worse in their panic to try to quash a kerfuffle. SendGrid wanted to run away from trouble as fast as possible to save their servers rather than protect their employee. Adria had a right to ask for civility at the conference, and, rather than insist on her right to do so, SendGrid fed the trolls by firing her.

Michal may have been out of turn in speaking about her organization's focus without permission; however, instead of getting rid of Michal and trying to run away from the conversation, the Federation could have used the enormous response Michal's blog post generated as an opportunity for a conversation about the future of Jewish life. Why make the principle worth fighting over in their organization the outdated notion of message control?

The leaders of these organizations showed the world that they valued peace and quiet, plans and profits, over principles and staffers. Looking out from their parapets, all they could see were attackers and threats, and immediately waved the white surrender flags.

Conclusion

Operating by principles enables organizations to focus more on Matterness and less on The Churn. Core principles become the basis for everything the organization does and how it operates. Organizations need to be organized around simple ideas that ensure that everyone inside and outside understands how the work is supposed to be done. The process of developing principles will unearth default settings that have assumptions about an organization's worldview. The absence of principles triggers micromanagement of staff by managers. The absence of principles focused on supporting staff can result in organizations turning their back on them when they most need protection.

Discussion Questions

- Do we have a set of fully articulated principles?
- Do these principles embrace Matterness?
- Are these principles widely shared with internal and external constituents?
- Are we using our principles or our plans to solve problems?
- Are we creating regular reflection time to assess our progress against both our plans and our principles?

Working With Crowds to Scale Matterness

THERE WAS A TIME WHEN organizations could safely assume that the people outside of their walls were passive audiences waiting to be told what to do. It may never have been a correct assumption, but it was a safe one, with few repercussions if constituents felt underserved or ignored. Social media freed individuals from this static arrangement by creating many more buying or donating options.

Today people will come and go as they please, not necessarily as organizations want them to. Social media can easily turn individuals into crowds that are visible, self-organizing, problem solvers, and great ambassadors for an organization. Learning how to create and manage crowds is a key skill for anyone trying to lead an effort. Crowds include constituents but also people passing by, rubberneckers, who may have a momentary interest and then move on to something else. Crowds are in constant motion, growing and shrinking all the time. Matterness is the glue that holds them together. Organizations need move from working alone to working with crowds, particularly if they want to scale their efforts.

This chapter outlines when and how crowds form, the ways organizations can work with them, and the many forms of new new capital — or "go-go juice" — that crowds can develop to support efforts. In addition, this chapter will describe ways that crowds can become co-creators and problem solvers with organizations.

Crowd Formation

For our purpose of understanding and scaling Matterness, a crowd is any gathering of people with a common purpose. For instance, individuals gather on a sidewalk to watch a performance artist. In the ten minutes they watch, the group becomes a crowd with a purpose, an audience for this performance. A small portion of that audience will become paying customers when they put a dollar in the open guitar case on the ground. That didn't just happen — the artist made it happen by performing and asking for donations. Another crowd gathers online to read a blog post — and, again, a few people in that crowd transition from spectators to active participants when they leave a comment. Crowds can form for fun, innocuous things, like sharing cat pictures, or important things, like overthrowing a government.

Working with crowds is not a one-way proposition of organizations asking people to do things for them. It requires organizations to open themselves up to the ideas, creativity, and resources of their constituents, people they don't pay or control. Fearless organizations follow as much as they lead their crowds. This is the fundamental reason why crowds are different from audiences.

The charge for organizations is to provide meaningful tasks for crowds to perform. "Meaningful" does not necessarily mean "arduous" or a lifetime of work, but the output of the work has to be useful and appreciated, not window dressing. Leaders need to figure out how to break down their overall efforts into bite-sized pieces to enable constituents to spend small bursts of time in helpful ways. This will take practice for most organizations. "Meaningful" could include commenting on a blog post, searching for earmarks within proposed legislation, commenting on proposed legislation, signing a petition and asking friends to do the same, providing feedback to an author on a proposal, or recording the oboe part of a Mozart sonata to be included in a video of an entire orchestra playing the piece. Meaningful work is visible, contributes to a larger effort, and can be used to encourage others to participate. A difficulty for some organizations working with crowds is remembering that crowds are made up of individuals who need and deserve to be treated like people not faceless members of a crowd. It is important that organizations are in conversation with their constituents to get their feedback and ideas for meaningful ways to contribute to an effort.

Leading crowds successfully takes clarity of purpose, intentionality, and some elbow grease. The steps outlined below presume that some effort has already been made to be in conversation with constituents and that some groundwork has already been laid to build a relationship of mutual benefit and trust between the organization and the crowd.

1. Understanding the Need. The first question to be answered is: Exactly what kind of "go-go juice" do we need? In other words, why is the crowd necessary? What can we do together to move our effort forward? I once asked a candidate for state senate what she most needed. She said, "$250,000." *That's odd,* I thought, *doesn't she need people to vote for her?* Too often, the reflexive answer people give when asked what they need is "money," and yet there are lots of different ways and kinds of capital that can meet their needs. There are lots of ways people can contribute their intelligence, networks, ideas, and even their empathy to an endeavor. A variety of different kinds of crowd-generated capital are outlined later in this chapter.

2. No Fakery. Organizations need to create fake-free zones and environments. Fake requests for help have become endemic within too many organizations. A fake request is: *Send me money today, or my opponent will win and send your children to Russia for kindergarten!* Or: *We need you to click "Like" on our Facebook page today! Because? Well, because we want you to.*

We have become experts at seeing through these artificial requests for help that are really just excuses to ask for donations and opportunities to capture our contact information. These are inside-out requests, with the only real benefit to the organization, not to the crowd. People need to be treated with dignity and respect, which means ensuring that their time and intelligence are respected and used well. Organizers need to think clearly about specific benefits to the crowd participants. Will there be a financial return, a burst of oxytocin from being generous, the feeling of accomplishment from creating a work of art together? Or maybe there will be all of these benefits.

3. Following and Leading. A crowd of purpose isn't born whole; it begins with a person's or organization's strongest ties and works outwards from there. Once constituents start to respond, then the rest of the crowd comes along, the friends of friends and strangers. Understanding what help is needed and asking for it in the right way are the critically important first step in a resource-rich ecosystem. However, there are times when the help an organization wants is different from what constituents want to give, and then the organization needs to follow rather than lead. Many online efforts, like the Ice Bucket Challenge in the summer of 2014, were started by individuals to support organizations like the ALS Association. Organizations need to be on the lookout for crowds that can enhance their efforts — but beware, these are not crowds to be "owned" by organizations.

4. Properly Asking for Help. People aren't going to give Procter & Gamble money to create a new product, but they may give money to Gary, a typical, budding young entrepreneur who emailed everyone he knows to try to raise $10,000 on Kickstarter for a new kind of mouse pad. And everyone he knows includes his mother's second cousin Martha and her second husband Henry. Gary's request is likely to create this conversation at Martha and Henry's kitchen table:

> *Henry, you remember Gary, don't you? He's Shelly's youngest son. Went to the University of Virginia, very smart. He has a new kind of mouse gizmo that Shelly says Apple Computer wishes they had thought of! He's trying to raise $10,000 on some website. Go ahead, Henry, give him a little money. No, more than that, make it $25. I'll call Shelly tomorrow and tell her we gave Gary a nice-sized donation for his thing.*

Gary never imagined his future would hinge on his mother's second cousin Henry donating $25 online. In order to get the "nice-sized donation," Gary had to swallow his pride and ask for help. Although it isn't easy for Gary to open himself up to the world and admit that he needs their help to make his dream come true, it is better than not taking a shot at realizing his dream. Gary needed to shift his thinking that asking for help is like asking for charity rather than an opportunity for his crowd to co-create something with him.

To make things more complicated, at the same time he asks for help, Gary needs to convey confidence that he is worthy of an investment. There is a sweet spot between vulnerability and vision that budding entrepreneurs like Gary need to find, and that may take a few tries.

Asking for a loan, investment, or donation will feel like asking for a handout if the asker doesn't do her homework and spadework. The homework is having a great story to tell about the new venture, what it will do, why it is needed, and how it will succeed. The spadework is keeping everyone apprised as the venture moves along, or gets stuck, and continuing to ask for advice, not just money. Gary needs to do his homework, take his best shot at appealing to his crowd for support, and, if it doesn't work, figure out what worked and what didn't by talking with his crowd — and do it again.

5. Reciprocity. Even if Gary uses a site like Kickstarter, where the contributions can be gifts rather than loans, Gary isn't getting the use of Henry's money for free. There are always expected returns from supporters. Generosity swells in a sea of reciprocity. Supporters need to be recognized and thanked quickly and genuinely for their efforts. The return doesn't have to be huge or expensive, but it does have to be heartfelt. A personal "thank you" goes a long way toward making someone feel appreciated and increasing the Matterness between the organization and that person. Gary could do something fun like gift-wrapping his first mouse pads and hand-signing them for supporters.

Showing real gratitude has too often been lost in The Churn. Individuals make up crowds, and they deserve to be thanked personally and individually. The thank-you form letter needs to go the way of the cassette tape. Whatever the gift is, personal attention to a gesture of gratitude is needed. Using someone's real name on a thank-you letter or perhaps adding a handwritten note at the bottom of a letter will have a huge impact. Very few organizations have so many thank you's to send that someone, somewhere cannot be bothered to write a personal note on it. And if it has to be a mass email, at least put some humility in it, something personal and meaningful that others will empathize with.

6. Trusting That Smart Answers Are in the Ecosystem. Being a smart leader like Henry Timms means saying, "I don't know the answer, but someone in this ecosystem does." Leaders need to become comfortable turning to their crowds as potential problem solvers. One mistake crowd leaders often make is assuming that every suggestion needs to be incorporated into their efforts. I have heard this expressed as "giving the store away to the amateurs." It's not nice to think about one's crowds as amateurs; it's also not accurate that asking for ideas and input is the same as acceding to all of them. The crowd leaders need to acknowledge which ideas and input are being used and why and thank everyone for their efforts. This is what it means to be in conversation with a crowd rather than broadcasting declarative statements.

7. Keep Talking to Your Crowd. It is critically important that leaders continue talking to their crowd after a request, including during any lulls in development. Too many organizations reach out to their constituents only in a crisis, and that wears thin very quickly. Ongoing community building is necessary to sustain efforts over a long period of time. Maybe it's an update on the project's progress or an update on one's personal journey. The crowd may lie fallow for a little while, and it may feel like the updates aren't really being appreciated. However, when the network is ready to go back into action, the nurturing will pay off.

There is a caveat for this last paragraph. Even if one continues to talk to a crowd and nurture it, some crowds aren't meant to last. As stated already, crowds come and go as they please, not as organizers necessarily want. Organizations that slide back into scarcity thinking believe that having contact information for a person makes this person "theirs" for a lifetime. Crowds created for a specific purpose have work to do, and, when the work is over, they simply go home. Leaders need to respect these feelings and begin to focus on creating another crowd.

Something has to happen to turn a group of people into a crowd with a purpose. That something is usually a story.

Stories That Energize Crowds

Stories often galvanize and connect people within crowds to a common purpose. Organizations often confuse testimonials with stories. *Fantastic service at this restaurant! Great selection of jeans at this store! Dr. Manny treated us like family! The Faceless Corporation met all of their deadlines on time!* So many testimonials, so little Matterness. Testimonials are about organizations; stories are about people.

A story is something personally felt, something that can move other people to understanding, empathy, revelation, and action. Stories are personal and passionate and reflect the interests and desires of constituents. The latest unemployment data don't go viral; the story of the stockbroker looking for work as a handyman does. Every organization has a lot of stories but just a few that are iconic — stories that perfectly reflect Matterness, the deep, personal connection between organizations and people. Iconic stories are timeless.

Dove Soap embraced Matterness with its Real Beauty campaign. There aren't many soap advertising campaigns that have their own Wikipedia pages, but this one does. The campaign is based on research that found that only 2% of women consider themselves to be beautiful. The first campaign efforts began in 2004. They were billboards featuring real women, with real curves, although with some editing of the photographs. Dove sales went up in 2005, in part because of all of the publicity surrounding the print campaign. The campaign continued with videos on the Dove website of mothers and daughters discussing beauty. Then, in the spring of 2013, the campaign went to another level with the Dove Real Beauty Sketches video.

It was more of a film than an advertisement. It was the story of a wide variety of women invited to meet with an FBI-trained forensic sketch artist. The artist asked the women to describe themselves so he could draw them. Then a new acquaintance of the women described them to the artist, and he drew another picture. The sketches as described by the women were less attractive than how they were described by a friend. The sketches shown side-by-side clearly illustrated the women's low self-esteem when it came to their own beauty. The tagline for the ad is, "You Are More Beautiful Than You Think."

At the time of this writing, the three-minute video had been viewed more than 58 million times and discussed on thousands of websites and millions of Facebook pages and tweets. While not all of the reaction was positive, this effort clearly demonstrates the importance of focusing on what customers are feeling — not just on what they should buy. This is what the ad folks call a brand-equity-building campaign. We feel better about Dove soap from watching the video. But did it sell soap? Dove's US sales went up 1% in the four weeks since the ad premiered, an incredibly difficult feat for a mature beauty product.

Stories are also powerful drivers for societal norms. In 1996, President Clinton signed the Defense of Marriage Act as a Gallup poll found that 27% of respondents were in favor of same-sex marriage. In 2006, Gallup found that 42% of respondents were in favor of same-sex marriage. In 2011, that figure rose to 53%, and by August 2014, 55% of Americans polled were in favor of same-sex marriage.

There are lots of factors involved in this kind of widespread societal shift. There have been legal changes that have overturned sodomy laws and made gay adoption legal. Television and movie stars like Ellen DeGeneres and George Takai coming out enabled their fans to see and accept famous, successful role models who also happen to be gay. Once it was legal and safe to be gay — once gay people became known and visible — their stories became easily shared and accepted. Everyone has a gay friend/cousin/coworker/child whom we see at work/parties/PTA/weddings, and now on online social networks. And many people have gay parents — including Zach Wahls.

On February 2, 2011, a video of a young man speaking in support of gay marriage was posted on YouTube. The video had a few hundred views when Moveon.org found it and posted it on their site six months later. It was an instant viral hit and has since garnered more than 17 million views on Moveon's site and another 2.8 million on YouTube. The star of the video, Zach Wahls, is a very handsome young man and a polished speaker, but what made this video particularly sticky was that he is not from New York City or San Francisco. Zach was speaking to the Iowa House of Representatives. His personal story demonstrated that same-sex families are no different from any other family. Zach's story provided fuel for the fast-changing same-sex marriage debates in state capitals across the country. This isn't "weird" or "coastal" or "out there" — it is in the heartland and normal.

There are powerful, iconic stories like these locked into every ecosystem. Organizations need to put their entire network on alert that they are looking for them. With enough practice, that iconic story — the one about the blind boy whose sight was restored through laser eye surgery, and the returning veteran whose uniform was cleaned for free by a local dry cleaner, and the little girl who had clean water for the first time in her life in rural Africa — becomes the story of the organization, too.

Organizers can put their story-galvanized crowds to work to generate a variety of different kinds of capital.

Different Kinds of Capital

We too often think of capital strictly in financial terms, but capital, or "go-go juice," is any resource that helps move an endeavor forward. Capital can be human connections, intelligence and expertise, resources like equipment and furniture, and, of course, money. Ideas and ventures that would have been improbable, impractical, or impossible in every previous century when capital was scarce are now probable, practical, and possible because of the social-media platforms that easily and inexpensively connect people with good ideas with people who want to support them. Capital doesn't just fly around; it leaves good stuff behind — trust. The more you experience reciprocity and generosity, the more you trust the better nature of other people.

The most remarkable aspect of the seismic shifts in the way that capital is being generated and shared isn't that it exists but that it took so long to get going.

Ebay was founded in 1995. Meetup has been around for more than ten years. They were enormous successes from the moment they pressed the "Go" button. It has already been proven many times over that people want to share, that they are overwhelmingly trustworthy, and that the Web is a great, friction-free platform for helping people connect with one another and distribute resources. And yet, we weren't marinating in capital even five years ago the way we are now.

So what changed?

The economy did. The Great Recession flattened the country. The most terrifying moment of the financial meltdown in 2007 was when banks froze. When banks stopped lending money, businesses couldn't make payroll, people couldn't make their mortgages, and the pistons of the nation's economy stopped pumping.

The changes in the economy smashed into the emergence of a host of social-media platforms that connect people in need of resources with those who have them. The resources include more than money — they include expertise, material goods like cars and couches, and even empathy.

The examples of different kinds of capital listed below all have the same fundamental building blocks. They have an online organizing hub, require a crowd to be successful, make progress toward a goal visible, have very low thresholds for participation, and they offer bite-sized ways to participate meaningfully over relatively short periods of time.

Financial Capital

Traditional banks deny 70% of small-business loans, and the rate is even higher for the "unbanked" — low-income people with no record of formal banking or credit history. Most people who wanted to start a small business or make a movie or record an album were shut out of the old economy. The advent and ease of crowdfunding have changed that.

Crowdfunding has reached a crescendo over the last few years as millions of people have participated online to give money to enterprising individuals. Kickstarter is one of the marquee crowdfunding sites enabling people to underwrite anything from a t-shirt business to a movie. According to Kickstarter's own statistics page, more than 66,000 projects have been successfully funded on the site, totaling more than $1.2 billion in funding. This is more than a 40% success rate for projects. Justin Kazmarck, the founder of Kickstarter, said, "Kickstarter is at the intersection of commerce and patronage; it's a way for creators and backers to bring a piece of work to life together."

Rewards for investors on these sites vary widely; some are philanthropic endeavors with no financial return, and some offer special gifts, such as a CD or t-shirt, for early investors. With the JOBS act of 2012, equity stakes are now available on crowd sites as well. The bottom line is that there has never been a time in the history of the world when so many creative ideas have come into contact with so many people willing to support them.

In 2005, Matt Flannery and Jessica Jackley created Kiva to take the idea of microenterprise to scale by matching entrepreneurs in developing countries around the world to donors online and making loans available to many more people than was previously possible. Donors were immediately enthusiastic about donating $25 to help a woman create a pottery shop in Kenya or helping a farmer in Peru replace his oxen with a tractor. And when that first loan was paid off, funders often rolled their donations into the next project. In the first year, more than $1 million was loaned. Today, Kiva raises more than $1 million a week to support projects around the world.

When the recession hit, Kiva was still going full blast internationally, but budding entrepreneurs in the US were finding it nearly impossible to get start-up funding. An idea that began as a way to help entrepreneurs in developing countries reversed course and came back home to the US.

The model in the US needed to be different because banks providing small-business loans exist here — they just don't work well for most people. Kiva decided to focus on "under-banked" individuals, those people being shut out of bank systems. Here is where the story gets new and interesting.

The US Kiva team asked themselves a question: "Without credit ratings, what would be a good substitute to indicate one's ability to pay back a loan?" Flipping open the playbook on all of the different forms of capital available to people, Kiva decided to rely on an applicant's social networks and character. People with good ideas and good character have no standing in the institutional financial capital system, but Kiva knew from its international work that these indicators matched exactly the success indicators for entrepreneurs around the world.

Requiring a character reference plus fifteen people willing to make loans has created a repayment rate to Kiva of 95 percent. The size of the loans is of no consequence; it can be as little as $5, but requiring one's own friends and family to vouch for a person and their idea immediately shifts the playing field. Instead of an individual negotiating with an institution, in an instant, that same person previously begging for a loan becomes an entrepreneur who is *known* in her network as a person with gumption trying to create something. Not only has the view of this person changed from the outside, their view of themselves changes — from a dreamer to a doer, from someone with no leverage, no access to the right people with money, to someone who matters to their own crowd and controls their own fate.

So, who are these fifteen people? Family members and friends, of course, but they're also something else. They tend to be geographically local. Not all of them, of course, but a majority of them are physically nearby and are as likely to have heard about the entrepreneur's efforts at the local coffee shop as online.

The importance of geography as a success factor isn't the sole domain of Kiva. According to Ethan Mollick, of the Wharton School, who studied more than 24,000 successful Kickstarter projects, local people were more likely to give to projects than people at a distance. This is particularly true for artistic projects, a mainstay of Kickstarter, where like-minded artists become critical supporters. This is why a city like Nashville has the lion's share of successful music-related Kickstarters. This jives with what we already know about living in Big Small Towns and innovation ping pong, where good ideas go up to the cloud, get support, and come back down to the ground.

A site called Crowdfunder has taken this dynamic further by connecting entrepreneurs to their local communities by organizing local pitch events. As Chance Barnett, the founder of Crowdfunder, wrote, "In short, big networks aren't the key to successful fundraising. Tightly knit, deep connections are."

The key components that make crowdfunding sites successful include quality ideas, of course, plus the creativity of the storytelling and the willingness and resilience the organizers to repeatedly ask friends and family for help.

Sharing Capital

The Web is serving as the neighborhood know-it-all, matching up people who have something extra to share, say, a spare bedroom or a car, with people in need. Contrary to what some people may believe, the boom in the sharing economy is not because it's a free-for-all, with people carelessly smashing together, but precisely because they aren't. Successful sharing sites are carefully managed experiences that inject their efforts with a certain amount of verifiability. By using just a few pieces of data, such as full name and address, the sites bridge the distance between stranger and acquaintance. Orchestrating exchanges of on-land goods and services is no place for anonymity. Using the few pieces of personal data as a starting point, most people are searchable online, and it's easy to find out where they work, whether they have been arrested, or have pictures on, say, Facebook, doing things you don't want done in your house. This is what Douglas Atkins calls "accelerated intimacy." Doug should know; he's the Global Head of Community at AirBnB.

AirBnB is an online platform that enables thousands of micropreneurs to turn an undercapitalized resource — their home — into a small business. People with a room or even a couch to spare are connected online with seekers of such spaces. This is not just a cute idea; it's a mega business that grew 300% in 2013. Turns out there are lots of people with a spare bedroom to rent — and also tree houses and castles and the entire country of Lichtenstein (street signs included)!

AirBnB is one of the most visible companies in the new and booming sharing economy, but there are dozens more. People are offering to share all sorts of resources, including cars, parking spots, and office space. Among many sharing-economy businesses, Uber and Lyft enable anyone with a car to become a taxi, and Homejoy provides housekeepers.

From a business perspective, these companies are exquisitely efficient. Their passionate participants find out about them through word of mouth or online, and they are easily and inexpensively scalable, with no languishing inventory and limited liability (participants sign waivers accepting responsibility for their own transactions).

Successful platforms are more than robotic matchmakers; they are "market curators" according to Anand Iyer, the Head of Product at Threadflip, an online consignment shop for clothes. Her site ensures that her users are known and safe by doing background checks. Site staffers ensure that the user experience online and on land is seamless, comfortable, and successful. Users are taught how to put quality photos of their clothes online. Higher-rated listings are shown first. Disastrous service providers are removed from the platform.

Homejoy, a service that matches housekeepers with clients, calls each unsatisfied customer to discuss their experience and figure out how to make future engagements go better not only for that customer but for others.

According to Jeremiah Owyan, the Chief Catalyst and Founder of the Crowd Companies Council, the sharing economy is driven by a variety of factors, including: denser populations that create more suppliers and demanders, and a desire for community and transactions that feel good and caring. The sharing economy resonates deeply with the Millennial Generation, our largest living generation that has recently come into adulthood. Their difficulty getting traction economically has resulted in their looking for alternative ways to build capital. They are also more willing to trust unknown people more than their parents. In a terrific summation of the long-term staying power of the sharing economy, Owyan quotes a banker as saying, "Access is more important than ownership."

As one would expect, the businesses being disrupted by the sharing economy are fighting back. Taxis are furious with Uber. Rental-car companies wanted to strangle Zip Car (including Avis, until they bought the company). Hotels would love for AirBnB to go away, and local governments, led by the New York State Attorney General's office, want to tax them like regular commercial hospitality.

Given the disproportional distribution of power between an upstart like AirBnB and the commercial-hospitality industry, backed by the almost-unlimited resources of industry lobbying groups and Attorneys General, chances are AirBnB will end up charging some kind of tax for each stay. However, it won't stop the growth of the sharing economy, because what can't be rewound or undone is the reality that people with resources can offer them to people in need online without traditional and expensive intermediaries. The platforms that serve as the matchmaker have found that people are eager to come together in relatively inexpensive and friction free ways.

Code as Capital

Software code has become important infrastructure for modern life. It is embedded in cars and computers, banks and supermarkets. Code enables us to move, know, share, connect, and learn from one another.

The history of computer code has followed two main threads: Code created for proprietary commercial products like the iPhone, and open-source code, created for the purpose of sharing with other coders, to be used and improved over time, such as code for Unix and Firefox. Open-source code is the ultimate abundant resource, used and improved through the generosity and ingenuity of coders who fervently believe that code is capital. Open-source code is completely agnostic; it isn't Republican or Democrat, and it isn't the province of a company or nationality. It is unisex, uniform, indelible ones and zeros that people can grab and use and improve and share back with the coding community. Open-source code can be capital that is much more than ones and zeros — it can also have a special history as it moves from project to project. Here is one story of code that keeps giving and going.

In October 2008, Nancy Scola and I were chatting at the end of a very intense presidential race. That election marked the coming-to-maturity moment for social media in a national election, particularly by the Obama campaign. Twitter, just two years old at the time and with about 3 million users, was just beginning the steepest part of its adoption curve. The use of Twitter as a political or civic tool had not yet been tested. What would happen, we wondered, if Twitter were used as an election-protection platform? Not as a campaign tool, but as a way for voters to share in illegalities like voter suppression or intentional misinformation. The goal was to give citizens the ability to report election fraud and manipulation in real time rather than report an incident after the fact to lawyers. *What could possibly be bad,* we thought, *about an idea that replaces lawyers with regular citizens?*

We threw the idea out to the blog readers at the Personal Democracy Forum site, where Nancy worked. "[F]or far too long, the job of election protection has fallen largely to lawyers schooled in election law. But there's an opportunity before us right now and through Election Day for thousands, if not hundreds of thousands, of citizens to identify and rectify voting problems in real time."

That's that, we assumed. We threw an idea into the vortex of the frenzied last days of a transcendent political season, where it would likely lie dormant. But it turned out to be just the opening chapter of a frantic campaign.

Bloggers and activists began to comment on the blog post. *Hell, yes,* they said. *C'mon, let's give it a try! We have a whole month to build this thing!* (Note: you may notice that coders have a different understanding of time from non-coders.) Within days, we had a group of about 40 people on board to create a new effort we called Twitter Vote Report. They were coders, advocates for fair elections, graphic designers, and general pot stirrers like Nancy and me.

In thirty days, our team of volunteers created a system called Twitter Vote Report that would pick up messages on Twitter with the hashtag of #twittervotereport and a zip code, draw them into a database, and map the tweets graphically and by problem type on the Twitter Vote Report website. This was an entirely voluntary effort, with no money spent on the development of the system. We watched with fascination and pride as the system rolled out across the country on November 4, 2008, Election Day. On that day, more than 12,000 election-protection messages were tracked by Twitter Vote Report. They detailed fake ballots that were passed out among waiting voters in St. Louis, voting machines that were broken in the Northeast, and the horribly long voting lines around the country.

The code powering Twitter Vote Report didn't materialize out of thin air; it was built, in part, using code developed three years before, during Hurricane Katrina. Andy Carvin, then at National Public Radio, helped create an online repository of information about available resources to respond to the hurricane. The code from that project helped undergird the Hurricane Information Center in 2008. The code was then used again in Twitter Vote Report with key people like Andy, Dave Troy, and Mike Turner, reusing, improving, and paying forward the code.

After Election Day 2008, Carvin and his fellow coders used the Twitter Vote Report code as part of Inauguration '09 to map and organize tweets for President Obama's first inauguration.

But the code still wasn't done.

On December 30, 2008, an election in Kenya pitted the opposition leader Raila Odinga against the incumbent Mwai Kibaki. Many Kenyans experienced voter intimidation and fraud during the election. Odinga supporters immediately cried foul. Protests and violence erupted around the country, reflecting decades of economic frustration. Over the course of the next few weeks, as gangs set fire to homes and blocked roads, 1,200 people were killed, and more than a million people were displaced from their homes or refugee camps.

Kenyans began to use text messaging and email to share stories about violence around the country, stories not being covered by the state-run newspaper and television station. A few enterprising volunteers decided that these digital messages could be aggregated and mapped. This effort became a nonprofit group called Ushahidi, meaning "witness" in Swahili. Ory Okolloh, a lawyer and one of the original volunteers, explained that Ushahidi started out as "an ad hoc group of technologists and bloggers hammering out software in a couple of days, trying to figure out a way to gather more and better information about the post-election violence." Okolloh asked for "any techies out there willing to do a mashup of where the violence and destruction is occurring, using Google

Maps" and said recording the truth of what was happening right at that moment would help the later process of reconciliation. Some of the code that Ushahidi hackers grabbed was from Twitter Vote Report. Two sleepless nights later, the map was up and being used by people inside and outside of Kenya.

Ushahidi has since been mapping political and natural crises around the world, from a Nigerian election, to the tsunami in Japan, to the earthquake in Haiti.

The code that began with Hurricane Katrina in 2005 has jumped around the world between organizations and people while being beholden to neither. It was available to and improved by people inside and outside of organizations. This kind of code is capital that powers efforts for justice (Ushahidi), commerce (Unix), search (Firefox), and civic life (Code for America).

Word of Mouth Capital

People consistently and overwhelmingly trust information about a product, a service, or a cause from a friend rather than from paid advertisements. Not only do people trust this information more, but 84% of respondents in a Nielsen survey say they act on this information more than on what they see or hear through paid advertisements. It certainly seems a good — and relatively inexpensive — bet for organizations to nurture and generate great word-of-mouth recommendations. Not only does this kind of capital help spread the word about good products and services, it also becomes free market research as people are talking about their efforts and providing ideas for ways to improve.

One way for organizations to turn their supporters into capital is by creating an ambassador program. Nicholas Norfolk is an avid runner. He is also a regular and enthusiastic brand ambassador for companies that serve runners like him. He doesn't do it to get rich or even to get free stuff (although that's not so bad); he does it to support a product or company that he admires. And he enjoys the experience. He says, "With the boom of social media, we find people that are genuinely excited and passionate about what they do. When they post, tweet, pin, or share, people listen." His advice for organizations is, "Quantity doesn't equate to being better. Make it a grassroots campaign. That will be more effective, in my opinion. Get a core group of ambassadors, and allow them to run wild. Allow them to build a community with the communities they are already a part of."

Since 2005, more than 10,000 people around the world have signed up to be Fiskateers. These are passionate crafters who enjoy activities like scrapbooking, card making, and quilting using Fiskar scissors and tools. They are invited to local events and demonstrations of Fiskar products, and they post patterns and designs on Pinterest boards. In 2009, one hundred Fiskateers were invited to Orlando, FL, to celebrate the company's 360th birthday. Kevin Briody wrote about this effort, "It is also a fantastic way for the company to hear directly from their most committed customers, creating a two-way dialogue that is the hallmark of smart ambassador programs."

Dignity Capital

We know that people are kind and generous by nature, but we haven't always had good mechanisms for being able to express our most empathetic selves. Megan Kashner is a social worker in Evanston, IL, just outside of Chicago. She founded the website Benevolent in 2011 as a way to put a human face on the real hardships of being poor in America. Her dream was to restore dignity to people trying very hard to gain traction in an unforgiving economy within a society that is increasingly unforgiving of the poor. In addition, as we saw in Chapter 1, "The Tyranny of Dichotomy," our society is increasingly separated by income, leaving fewer places for people of different incomes to get to know one another. Putting an individual human face on the struggles of low-income people enhances their Matterness and enables them to be seen and heard more in a world in which they are so often overlooked and marginalized.

On Benevolent, low-income people tell their own stories and ask for a little help. The stories are verified by a network of local nonprofits Megan is in partnership with to help prepare and support the individuals in need. Jose has a new job in a restaurant but can't afford the black pants and shirt that are required of employees to wear. Jennifer has her first apartment with her two-year-old and needs some basic furnishings. Calista needs dentures; otherwise, she is unemployable. Requests generally total in the low hundreds of dollars. These stories are heartbreaking in their simplicity and humbling for the viewer who may never have struggled in these ways. People responded immediately to these stories, as Megan hoped they would, with generosity of spirit and donations and perhaps a whisper to themselves of, "There but for the grace of God go I."

At the other end of the independence spectrum from the askers on Benevolent is Amanda Palmer, a musician who instinctively understood from the beginning of the social web that her relationship with her audience had changed. Her music is a cross between punk and cabaret — not for everyone, she recognizes, but certainly for enough people to fuel a career. She is in constant communication with her passionate supporters through her blog and Twitter. Amanda is just one part, one "node," in network lingo, of a larger community of people who are passionate about her kind of music. Being in conversation with one another has changed their roles. Amanda doesn't think of her fans as a passive audience sitting back and waiting to buy an album or a ticket to a concert, and her fans don't think of her as a distant and unreachable performer. When she sends out a message on Twitter that she is in, say, Berlin, her community brings her food, offers their couches to sleep on, and comes to hear her music.

She tried the major-music-label route in 2008 for an album called *Who Killed Amanda Palmer?* What Amanda viewed as a successful debut of her album released by Roadrunner Records, with more than 25,000 records sold in the first few weeks, was immediately deemed disappointing by the label. Amanda's definition of success and the label's were not compatible.

What to do?

Amanda knew there was dignity to be uncovered by doing what she does best: Making the music she loves and relying on her community to support her. It was a way for her to own her artistry rather than settle for being a pawn of a record company. She recalls, "I decide I'm going to give my music away for free whenever possible....but I'm going to ask for help....I fell into those thousands of connections I had made, and I asked my crowd to catch me." Amanda created a campaign on Kickstarter with the hopes of raising $100k to record her next album. She raised $1.2 million from 25,000 people instead, presumably many of whom had bought the studio album and would rather see their money go to Amanda than a record company. Skeptics ask her, "How did you make all these people pay for your music?" She answers, "I didn't make them — I asked them, and through the very act of asking them, I connected with them. When you connect with them, people want to help you."

Amanda's passive consumers had turned into an active crowd with a purpose, using their leverage and generosity to ensure that their money went exactly where they wanted it to go. Anyone can download music online for free, and millions of people will continue to do that. But then there are other people, Amanda's people, who want to support independent artists — and independent workers.

Kronda Adair is a coder who wanted to go to the Lesbians Who Code national conference, but, after a year of bad health, she couldn't afford it. She turned to Indiegogo and created a campaign to raise $1,000 to ask people to underwrite her conference registration and expenses. Within four hours, her campaign had hit the original goal, and, after a week, she had raised $1,486. Why would so many people support a business expense? Because Kronda's friends knew her story and wanted to help. Kronda said, "I had 25 funders, about half of whom are friends, ranging from people I went to high school with, long-time personal friends, college classmates, and people I met more recently at conferences or on Twitter." But not everyone was a personal friend; the other half were friends of friends. Upon reflection, Kronda said, "It feels great that so many people were eager to help, share the word, and generally get excited with and for me. I think it's a good indicator that my efforts to live a life that is generally helpful to others have been at least somewhat successful."

Crowds can be enormously helpful solving a problem that has already been identified. They can also be just as helpful creating new efforts and identifying and solving problems together with organizations.

Co-Creation and Problem Solving

Crowds with a purpose create the opportunity for co-creation and problem solving. This is how organizations will become more sustainable in the future. But in order to be creative problem solvers, people have to be given real problems to solve.

Co-creation, like old age, Peter C. Verhoef, Sander F.M. Beckers, and Jenny van Doorn warn, "...is not for the fainthearted. It involves a fundamental transformation of the firm's operating model and needs to start with top management's commitment." The authors describe an experiment at BD Worldwide, an international biomedical company. The senior management team decided to empower the sales representatives to go beyond just selling products to be in conversation with hospital staff to better understand their work and their problems. These conversations yielded immediate positive results. For instance, they learned how and why the spread of infection by dirty needles continued in hospitals. The sales team then fed this information to the product team to design a new needle cover. This internal process of co-creation remade the role of the sales people from the frontlines for transactions to a trusted advisor and relationship builder between the company and hospitals.

Co-creators can be a crowd of one and still be effective. New York City government has invited independent coders to take city data and turn it into whatever products they want. John Krause grabbed an enormous set of police data in his spare time and created Crashmapper to analyze and visualize the most dangerous intersections in New York City. Krause created this software, "in my spare time over a long period of time — three weeks."

Spartan Race is a company that turns obstacles into opportunities for its participants. Everyone knows that life is filled with obstacles, big ones like illness and death, and small ones like long lines at the snack counter at the movie theatre and fender benders. Our obstacle-filled worlds can be emotionally exhausting as we often careen from one struggle to the next. Spartan Race's co-founder, Joseph DeSena, takes life's obstacles as an insult to his ability to overcome nearly anything put in his way. As a hard-driving former Wall Street executive, he lives by the motto, "Death is the price we pay for life, so make it worth it."

Spartan Race, started in 2005, has the kinds of grueling obstacle courses made for Marines, and yet stockbrokers, advertising executives, stay-at-home moms, people recovering from illness and car accidents flock to these races. The Spartan Race obstacle courses are difficult in an almost video-game-like way as racers crawl over barbed wire, jump over fire, and swim through mud. The goal, DeSena says, is to be uncomfortable and overcome obstacles, literally and figuratively, in order to find out what a person is capable of doing when challenged. He believes that pushing oneself to the limits of physical and emotional exhaustion is a rebellion against our culture of obesity and technology-fueled laziness. The mandatory wavier for participants in the toughest Spartan Race is one line, "I may die."

One man lost 270 pounds to prepare for the race. Couples have met their life partners at races. Other have overcome their own physical limitations or learned to live full lives with a disease. The idea of actually overcoming obstacles is life affirming for many of the participants.

What started as a $5,000 investment in a single race almost ten years ago has turned into 130 races in 2014 held in 17 countries. They have added races for individuals with special needs and veterans who have lost limbs.

The phenomenal growth of Spartan Race isn't just because of the races — it is because of the intense relationship the organization creates with the racers. Although races are an act of rebellion against technology, the organization thrives because of its online ecosystem that turns racers from customers into co-creators. Joseph spent every day answering email and talking to participants on Facebook about the race experience and how to improve it for the first three years. He and his colleagues continue to be in conversation with participants. Spartan Race doesn't operate *at* its own racers, but *with* them, constantly, in real-time and over time. Powerful stories are shared online after races about the immense mental and physical challenges participants have overcome. As a result, Spartan Race has nearly 4 million Likes on its Facebook page.

Participants are individuals, not numbers on jerseys, to Spartan Race. The organization spends an enormous amount of time thinking about the races from the outside-in. They look at the race experience through the eyes of the participants to communicate where to go and what to expect, to ensure that food and water are easily and abundantly available to the racers, and that the sites are cleaned up and a space is created for celebration afterwards. In return, Spartan Race participants are the organization's best marketers for recruiting new racers.

Unfortunately, too often, organizations want to keep problem solving private and hidden. Problem solving is generally considered an internal activity, not something to be aired publicly. It can even feel shameful for some staff who feel that they should know all of the answers. When leaders understand that vulnerability is a strength, not a weakness, then public problem solving becomes a resource, not a demerit.

Not every problem-solving effort has to be as big and long as these. There are everyday problems that could be taken public. Here is an example of how it works.

A complaint about Sally's Fitness Club is posted on Yelp: "I showed up for my workout at 6:30 am, and the doors were still locked."

Instead of the pro forma "So sorry we disappointed you" response, Sally and her staff bring the complaint to their blog or Facebook page and post it with this explanation: "Morning, everyone. Marcie W. posted this on Yelp last night. We did change our hours a month ago because we couldn't afford to open that early and stay open longer at night, as we heard people wanted us to. What do you think? Should we keep to the new hours? Should we have a few days a week when we open early and close a little earlier at night?"

Some people weigh in that they like the new hours, and others miss the early hours. Sally and her staff respond to some of the comments ("Thanks, Joe; I hadn't thought of having coffee on the house on our extra early days.") and discuss the results internally while looking at their staffing and budget issues. There are 14 people in favor of keeping the hours the same but 37 who want the gym to open early a few days a week, say, Monday and Wednesday. Sally comes back the next day with this post: "Hi, everyone. Thanks so much for weighing in on the hours issue yesterday. If you're keeping score at home, you'll know that we had 14 people in favor of keeping the hours the way they are and 37 in favor of having two early days a week. We'd like to propose an experiment for the next three months of trying early hours on Monday and Wednesday. Please let me know how you think the new system is working."

In addition, taking the problem truly public, not just to a members-only group, enables non-members to weigh in as well. This would have been anathema to the old-school thinking that only members count in decision-making about the gym. However, this is an outstanding way to recruit new people interested in belonging somewhere where their voices can be heard. Or maybe some other smart person just has a good idea — why not listen to it?

Of course, if Sally felt like there were many more people who needed to weigh in on this question, she could also send out a survey. However, if the data-collection process takes too long and is too complex, the energy Sal is creating by going immediately to her online community and asking for help will be lost. Something tangible, real, and personal becomes sanitized and distant through a survey.

Public problem solving creates a few more benefits. It creates a far more committed core of people invested in helping Sally make her gym work for the entire community. Working this way shows the world that the organization is aware of problems and complaints and takes them seriously. Even if you were not the complainer, it shows you how Sally and her staff treat complainers — with respect and as open-minded listeners, not defensive automatons. And, of course, it puts to rest the erroneous assumption that only staff can or should solve problems. There are lots of smart people out there who are happy to offer ideas or links to resources, or just to commiserate ("That's a tough one, Sal, but you have my membership whichever way you go.").

A missed opportunity for public problem solving was the Obama administration's development of Healthcare.gov. Rather than the traditional Beltway Bandit, lowest-bidder route, the administration could have chosen an open-source approach. This approach would have required contracting to a central coordinator who would be responsible for adopting code created by other people around the country, or even the world. In particular, the general contractor could have called upon the myriad coders in Silicon Valley and Alley who were chomping at the bit to participate in this project. I wrote shortly after the web site had its disastrous debut, "But it's not just the coding that could have been different with Healthcare.gov; the greatest loss is the persistent disempowerment of our citizenry. The administration's focus is on risk reduction. While trying to tightly control processes and communications is understandable for an administration that has had to withstand daily assaults from critics, the cost of allowing critics to dictate how the administration operates leaves the rest of us on the sidelines."

After the initial debacle of the website, the white-hat programmers who rode to the rescue were exactly the people who wanted to help in the first place but were shut out of the initial, insular process. As Gabriel Burt, one of the rescue-team members, said afterwards, "The two months I spent on this were harder and more intense than the 17 months I spent on the campaign... But I loved every minute of it...I believe in getting people health care. I am so proud of this."

Conclusion

Because people within crowds are going to come and go constantly, creating opportunities for new people to easily engage in meaningful ways ensures that an organization continues to replenish its crowd. Matterness is the constant in these engagements — the willingness of organizations to reach outside of their walls for input, advice, and help connected to large numbers of people willing to contribute their smarts, networks, money, and ideas.

Discussion Questions

- Exactly what kind of capital do we need to reach our goals? Do we need smart people, a shared space, intelligence, creativity, partners?
- Who could be our ambassadors, and what could we do together?
- Are you prepared to ask for real help?
- Are we talking to our crowd when we don't need their immediate help?

Action Cascades of Matterness

ALMOST EVERYBODY WHO HAS ever posted something online hopes it will become an instant sensation. Going viral is not a number of viewers but a viewing effect. It means that strangers of the original content are sharing it. In other words, there is no additional marginal cost to the creator for additional people to see or share it. This is unlike broadcast media, where the originator has to pay for more airtime or ad space for more eyeballs to fall on their message. Going viral means that something is being shared widely — it doesn't necessarily mean that any action was taken. Ideas and images that go viral are called cascades. Cascades can lead their own life, a fun-fulled cat video making the rounds, or a heart-warming picture sent from mothers to their children. Cascades can also become something else, action cascades, when built-in small actions are taken by crowd members to influence ideas, advocate for justice, donate to a cause, or buy a product. These action cascades are by definition filled with Matterness.

This chapter will describe cascades and action cascades and their anatomy. It will also describe what happens when cascades take a wrong turn and become mobs.

Cascades

The overwhelming number of online posts, photos, and videos are not shared with anyone. One researcher estimates that only 5% of all photos uploaded to Facebook are shared by other people. The top .05% of photos shared make up 50% of the total number of photos reshared. However, when an idea, or image, or story begins to travel through social networks, the resulting cascades are impossible to ignore.

Mike Braff was riding on the Q subway train on October 31, 2013. It was a very ordinary ride until Braff saw an extraordinary act of kindness. When he got home, Braff posted a photo on Reddit and wrote, "Heading home on the Q train yesterday when this young black guy nods off on the shoulder of a Jewish man. The man doesn't move a muscle — just lets him stay there. After a minute, I asked the man if he wanted me to wake the kid up, but he shook his head and responded, 'He must have had a long day — let him sleep. We've all been there, right?'"

Braff later said, "I just thought it was a sweet picture and really encapsulated the New York that doesn't get shown a lot." Someone else cross-posted the photo to Facebook, where it quickly received more than 20,000 Likes. The mainstream media then picked up the story, and outlets like Huffington Post and local television news made the online sharing of the photo go into hyperdrive. The photo has been viewed more than 1.2 million times as of this writing.

Braff's photo was a lovely reminder that we live in a world filled with grace that we don't celebrate often enough. The photo became an instant viral cascade wherein people passed along the information from one to another; hubs of influence like news outlets picked it up, and then it kept on going. As Christaki and Fowler wrote in *The Connected*, "...once networks are established, altruistic acts — from random acts of kindness to a cascade of organ donation — can spread through them."

Karen Klein was riding a school bus filled with middle-school children in Greece, NY, on June 19, 2012. Karen had been safely delivering children to and from school for twenty-three years, the first twenty as a driver and the last three as a bus monitor. But as much as that Tuesday was like any other day on the bus, it was also profoundly different. The yelling and taunting that routinely occurs on school buses across the country spiraled out of control that day, and rather than aiming their cruel verbal fusillades at one another, three seventh-grade boys aimed it at Karen — and a fourth videotaped it on his cell phone.

The video was posted on Facebook and on YouTube. Friends began to tell friends about it, and soon thousands of people had seen the video. Two days later, Karen was on the *Today Show* discussing the incident and how violated she felt. By the time the interview ended, millions of people had viewed the video online. In an instant, the verbal assault that left a 68-year-old, widowed, partially deaf woman in tears had catalyzed a national conversation about teenagers and bullying.

The same day that Karen was talking to Matt Lauer, Max Sidorov, a nutritionist in Toronto, heard the story on his local TV news. He immediately set up a fundraising site on Indiegogo.com to support Karen. "Let's raise $5,000 and send Karen on vacation," he posted. Max announced his fundraising campaign on his Facebook page by writing, "She doesn't earn nearly enough ($15,506) to deal with some of the trash she is surrounded by. Let's give her something she will never forget — the vacation of a lifetime!"

Max turned Karen's cascade into an action cascade by giving people something important and immediate to do.

After two hours, the Indiegogo campaign exceeded Max's $5,000 goal. But donors kept giving money. By the end of the first day, $100,000 had been raised. The mainstream media reported on Max's success, a passionate Reddit sub-group shared it, and the total kept rising. After a month, Max had raised more than $700,000 from more than 32,000 people around the world. Karen is now a retired bus monitor.

Remember the thermometers in town centers used to track donations for annual campaigns? Those thermometers were filled in using red marker, say, weekly, to show progress against the campaign's goal. Max's campaign also had a thermometer, but, because this one was online, it was visible, updated in real-time, and easily sharable among friends. In addition, Max's effort had all the key elements found in similar successful online fundraising efforts: A sticky story (one that is rooted in emotion and easy to explain), a sympathetic victim, vicious villains, real-time video of the event, and scalability.

But there was still a mystery about Max's campaign. Why did so many people give so much money beyond the original goal of $5,000? Clearly the intended outcome had already been met at $100,000, $250,000, and certainly at $500,000, and yet people kept giving. They gave because it felt good to help Karen. They also gave because they remembered being bullied as children or watching someone else being bullied. There was still another reason. Stephen Reicher, a psychology professor at Scotland's University of St Andrews, explained the outpouring of support for Karen by saying, "It often helps if it's turned into something concrete and embodied. To say lots of people are suffering is an abstract concept. To see this one woman suffering, and to be able to help her is more concrete."

This was the key to Max's fundraiser and to all action cascades — providing just the right action at just the right time. The actions in an action cascade have to be easy, fast, and emotionally satisfying.

Isaac Thiell's spontaneous act of loving kindness of lending his shoulder to a tired young man on the subway could have become an action cascade if meaningful actions had been available for the people who viewed the photo. Someone like Max could have posted the photo on Pinterest and asked others to share photos of similar acts of loving kindness. Someone else could have created a Facebook group dedicated to acts of grace that are too often overlooked and asked members to post an inspiring photo a day.

In order for an action cascade to form, something needs to happen beyond viewing a video. This may seem painfully obvious, but, too often, organizations get so enamored of a message going viral that they forget that they are in the business of selling a product. For instance, Claude Van Damme starred in an online ad for Volvo trucks. In the video, Van Damme is straddling two trucks as they drive down the highway. The video was watched more than 70 million times but translated into only 83,902 followers on its YouTube channel. The Old Spice ads featuring Isaiah Mustafa were a huge sensation, and, initially, sales went through the roof, with a more-than 100% increase in sales over the previous year's corresponding quarter. However, according to one analyst, "there were so many buy-one-get-one-free coupons for Old Spice body wash that it swamped the impact any advertising could have." The following year, with subsequent videos still being widely watched, sales were down significantly when the coupons were no longer offered. These ads pulled in eyeballs, but they didn't open wallets. Tara Hunt, a social media expert, wrote of such campaigns, "...the definition of a successful campaign that focuses on quantity means the focus will be on achieving enormous numbers of views, retweets, or shares." She continued, "Viral is a zero-sum game on a medium that is about community, not competition."

Action cascades are more than viral hits — they are a crowd working in concert toward a common goal, like Max's campaign. They are often spontaneous events, but they can also be purposefully created if one understands their anatomy.

Anatomy of Action Cascades

An action cascade is a very large event that requires a specific structure for success. They have three parts: organizers, doers, and rubberneckers. As with any human endeavor that requires organization, a few people are organizers, more are doers, and still more are rubberneckers.

Organizing is a lonely job. The **organizer**(s) does far more work than anyone else — they always have, and they always will. Organizers define the purpose of the crowd, find a venue, cajole others into helping out, and send out the reminders. They are the hosts of the party, the mother of the bride, the troop leader, and the project manager. Social media provide the opportunities for anyone, anywhere, inside and outside of organizations, to act as organizers.

Organizers can have an idea ahead of time, or they can see that a crowd is gathering that can be made purposeful. Organizers provide actions that others can run with and ensure that the effort stays on track. Wendy Harman, the head of social media of the American Red Cross, is just such an organizer.

On January 12, 2010, an enormous earthquake devastated Haiti. Whole neighborhoods collapsed into rubble. It was immediately clear that the rescue and clean-up effort would require enormous resources from the world. In a day, the American Red Cross was making donations available by text message. In a few weeks, they had raised more than $35 million by text — a record amount. But anyone who knows about the complex logistics of organizing a text giving campaign knows that one day wasn't enough time to get an effort like this up and running. Wendy certainly knew this — which is why she had spent the previous nine months preparing to use text giving for whatever large-scale disaster came next. Wendy was the organizer of the effort, ready to press the "go" button with an easy and emotionally satisfying action.

But even Wendy, with all of the resources of the American Red Cross, needed **doers** between her and the donors to make her effort take off. Wendy's doers were mainstream media and influential bloggers. For a strapped start-up venture, the doers are often family members and close friends putting posters up on telephone poles at midnight and calling their friends to ask them to come to the grand opening of their store. These are the people who not only tell their neighbors about a sale or an action cascade but also email their friends and family about it and post it online. Too often, organizations assume that doers need to be paid staff. Over and over again, people have shown a willingness to share news, information, tools, and opportunities with their friends online with no reward other than feeling good about themselves or burnishing their reputations as trusted sources of information.

Rubberneckers are the final piece of the cascade anatomical puzzle. Rubberneckers have a bad reputation for slowing traffic down to a crawl to see how badly a car is crushed in the other lane during rush hour, but they serve a vital purpose for cascades. Rubberneckers are vital to action cascades, because, using social media, they can so easily transition from watching to doing. Rubberneckers tell the rest of us to pay attention to something. The ability of casual passersby to power action cascades is why the digital ecosystem is so expansive. Friends or even strangers recommending something by email or Facebook or on a site like Yelp are far more influential in our decision making than impersonal, mass-market ads.

It is easier to activate online rubberneckers than on-land rubberneckers, but, because it is so easy, it is also easy to dismiss them as unimportant. Online rubberneckers are often derisively called "slactivists." This isn't true, accurate, or fair. Online activists aren't lazy or ineffective. One study found that signing an online petition increased the likelihood of the signer giving money to that cause in the future. Another study found that online activists were twice as likely to volunteer in other civic actions, four times more likely to encourage writing a letter to the government, and six times more likely to sign a petition than people who do not participate in online activism.

The job of organizers is to create activities that will energize doers to activate rubberneckers. These activities are generally immediate, small, and visible to the world online. Here are a few stories of action cascades in action.

Action Cascades in Action

Dan Savage lives in Seattle, WA, writes a sex column called "Savage Love" and hosts a podcast called the Savage

Lovecast. In the fall of 2010, Dan was reading about a rash of teen suicides around the country. In September 2010, Tyler Clementi, a gay freshman at Rutgers University, had a romantic interlude secretly videotaped by his roommate. His roommate, Dharun Ravi, added injury to insult by posting the video online. Shortly thereafter, Tyler committed suicide by jumping off the George Washington Bridge. At about the same time, a gay teenager, Brandon Bitner of Middleburg, PA, ran in front of a truck at 3 am and killed himself. These incidents reminded Dan of his own struggle as a teenager who was bullied because he was gay.

"I wish I could have talked to those kids for five minutes before they committed suicide to tell them it gets better," Dan told me in December 2010. "I was stewing on that and realized I was waiting for permission in an era when I didn't need it anymore — I had YouTube and Twitter and Facebook, and I could go over the heads of the parents, preachers, and teachers of these bullied kids who are isolated and lonely and scared and directly address them."

Dan and his husband, Terry Miller, went to a bar owned by friends and shot a video. There wasn't a script — it was just a conversation about how they felt being bullied and how much better it feels to be a gay adult than a gay teen. They uploaded the video the next day to YouTube and called it *It Gets Better.*

Dan used his print column and his podcast to announce the video. In addition to encouraging people to watch the video and share it with others, he also encouraged them to make their own videos. In just a few days, more than 250,000 people had viewed Dan and Terry's video, and many of the watchers sent Dan their own videos. Within six days, Dan posted 1,000 videos to the *It Gets Better* YouTube channel. YouTube expanded his limit to 5,000 videos. Thousands of people around the country were sending him videos, watching the videos on his channel, and talking about them online, on mainstream media, and in schools.

This was the first instance of a YouTube *channel* going viral. The first 1,000 videos were gay people talking about their own experiences, like Dan and Terry, and then celebrities like Lady Gaga and politicians like President Obama and Hillary Clinton jumped in without invitation. Dan reflected on the amazing success of the *It Gets Better* video channel: "When we gave ourselves permission to talk to them and then gave everyone else permission to talk to them, people just jumped in...we're having this moment of cultural awareness of the heightened risk of suicide for LGBT kids...and the moment will pass, and these videos will still be accessible; they'll still be doing the job of helping these kids and raising awareness because they're not going into dresser drawers — they're going to live forever online on YouTube and on our site."

The online videos for the *It Gets Better* Project were just a beginning. The Project continues by creating and distributing curricula for schools to download and use to discuss the issue, a great integration of online and on-land resources and actions.

A hashtag can stimulate a cascade as well as a video. A hashtag is akin to a tab on a file folder; its only purpose is to organize information online. If you want to know what people are saying right now about the Knicks or President Obama or global climate change, you can search and follow the posts by using a hashtag.

"Let's create a national day of giving on the Tuesday after Thanksgiving on par with Black Friday and Cyber Monday. We'll call it #GivingTuesday." What agency or politician or company or rock star proclaimed unto us this day of giving in 2012? Henry Timms did. Remember

Henry Timms, he is the executive who learned how to become vulnerable with his staff. He is a British ex-pat who was the assistant executive director of the 92nd Street Y in Manhattan. In concert with the United Nations Foundation, Henry decided it was time to push back against the ceaseless commercialization of the holiday season by creating an opening day for an entire season of giving. Henry organized a circle of doers, who began to attract nonprofit organizations who also wanted to spearhead a national day of giving. What should they do on this day of giving? Whatever they wanted to do, said Henry — that's why the day begins with a hashtag.

#GivingTuesday is open to anyone participating in any way they want. The idea caught on immediately across the country. Messages zipped around for weeks before and after that Tuesday. *Let's raise $10,000 to match what a donor said he'd give that day. Let's all gather at the community center and make sandwiches for homeless people. Let's each give $25 to provide seeds for farms in Africa.* Lots and lots of people were saying, "Let's put on a show," and their doers and rubberneckers said, "Count me in."

On #GivingTuesday the event bounced from online to on land and back again, with photos and updates of events taking place at food banks, community shelters, and theaters around the country. At the end of the day, Henry and his fellow organizers would have been thrilled if 50 organizations had raised $100,000. Instead, more than 2,500 nonprofits (an increase of 53% from the previous Tuesday after Thanksgiving) reported raising more than $10 million. Astoundingly, more than 60% of the donors to #GivingTuesday were first-time donors to causes and gave because an online friend asked, and those were the rubberneckers with something good to do with their time and energy. The following year, more than 10,000 organizations around the world participated in #GivingTuesday, raising more than $19 million. Giving was up 90% over the previous year, the average online gift was up $40, and the hashtag #GivingTuesday was tweeted as much as 700 times per minute!

Action cascades are effective to get people to do not only easy things but hard things as well. Sadly, many Americans find it too cumbersome, unimportant, or hard to vote. Scholars at the University of California, San Diego, tried an experiment to increase voting turnout through Facebook during the 2010 elections. They posted nonpartisan "get out the vote" ads at the top of the news feeds of 60 million Facebook users. The message included a link to a polling-place finder and a counter of how many Facebook users reported voting already. It also included pictures of up to six Facebook friends who reported voting. One percent of these users were randomly chosen not to have the picture of their friends included in the message. Another 600,000 users did not receive a message and were used as a control group.

The group with pictures of their friends in the ad was more likely than the other two groups to click on the "I Voted" button. But, of course, we know that people sometimes say they voted when they didn't, especially when other people are looking. The researchers compared the "I Voted" group to public records of who voted and found that they, indeed, voted at a higher rate than those who didn't receive the photos of friends who voted. James Fowler, the lead researcher, wrote, "The main driver of behavior change is not the message — it's the vast social network. Whether we want to get out the vote or improve public health, we should focus not only on the direct effect of an intervention but also on the indirect effect as it spreads from person to person to person."

Just as there are good witches and bad ones, there are good crowds and bad ones. Online crowds can easily turn into hateful mobs with the same structure as action cascades aimed as often at regular people as at athletes, celebrities, and politicians. These hateful cascades leave a trail of shattered psyches and ruined reputations behind them.

A Tale of Two Tarts (or When Crowds Become Mobs)

Anyone can go online and shout at people who have wronged them using social media, whether it is an unfaithful husband being called out by his wife, the rude shoe sales clerk who wouldn't accept the returned shoes bought yesterday, or the public official caught on video cursing at a constituent. We can watch, share, and shout from the rooftops that this person should be fired or this politician recalled from office, or that this company should go out of business. And most of these shouts will simply come and go in the course of a day. However, there are other times when the public shaming of a person turns into a cascade. There is an important line between justified shaming and vengeance that social media easily enables crowds to cross. This leads us to one of the most frightening parts of living in a digital world: The fast and ferocious creation of angry mobs.

Here are two stories of viral hate unleashed online against individuals.

"A Tale of Two Tarts" was written by Monica Gaudio in 2005 and posted on the Gode Cookery blog. It was not an article about two women with dubious reputations but a discussion of two medieval apple-pie recipes. In October 2010, Gaudio noticed that her article was used without attribution in *Cooks Source* Magazine, a small New England publication. According to a blog post by Gaudio, she sent several emails to the magazine asking for an apology and recompense of $130 in the form of a donation to the Columbia School of Journalism. Again according to Gaudio, the magazine editor, Judith Griggs, responded by email with a message that included this paragraph:

"Yes, Monica, I have been doing this for 3 decades, having been an editor at *The Voice, Housitonic Home,* and *Connecticut Woman* Magazine. I do know about copyright laws. It was "my bad" indeed, and, as the magazine is put together in long sessions, tired eyes and minds sometimes forget to do these things. But honestly, Monica, the Web is considered 'public domain,' and you should be happy we just didn't 'lift' your whole article and put someone else's name on it! It happens a lot, clearly more than you are aware of, especially on college campuses and in the workplace. If you took offense and are unhappy, I am sorry, but you, as a professional, should know that the article we used, written by you, was in very bad need of editing and is much better now than it was originally. Now it will work well for your portfolio. For that reason, I have a bit of a difficult time with your requests for monetary gain, albeit for such a fine (and very wealthy!) institution. We put some time into rewrites — you should compensate me! I never charge young writers for advice or rewriting poorly written pieces, and I have many who write for me…ALWAYS for free!"

Them's Internet fightin' words. A story on NPR about this incident said it had three things that produce an instant Internet firestorm: misinformation, disrespect for creative people, and jaw-dropping condescension.

Ron Doyle describes what happened next: "Within 48 hours of the story's release, digilantes had compiled a document listing more than 150 alleged cases of misappropriation, plagiarism, and copyright infringement against *Cooks Source* magazine. Among those were articles taken from authors at NPR and The Food Network, the latter of whom has allegedly begun an investigation into the matter. Some advertisers have dropped the magazine, siding with Gaudio and the Internet mob. At this moment, the *Cooks Source* Facebook page has more than 5,600 'fans' (up from an estimated 110 before the debacle) and, by my rudimentary calculations, is receiving an average of 40 complaints, insulting jokes, and sarcastic comments every minute."

This mob included a lot of people who were appalled and incensed by Griggs' patronizing, insensitive, and flat-out wrong response regarding copyright and the Web. And many of those people expressed themselves on the *Cooks Source* Facebook page and Gaudio's blog. These are two typical comments from readers of Monica's blog post:

"You just became my WTF link of the day. I feel so much outrage on your behalf, and I hope this is resolved to your benefit.

"The thought of someone stealing someone else's words is just rage inducing; I can't even elaborate further without dissolving into curses."

Within just a few weeks, advertisers quickly peeled away, and *Cooks Source* closed its doors.

It seemed to many observers that Griggs received the punishment she deserved. But there have been many other victims who didn't deserve to be singled out — much less become the focal point of a viral mob.

Lisa Khoury was a sophomore at The University at Buffalo in February 2012 when she wrote her first opinion piece for *The Spectrum*, the school newspaper. She took the con side in the question of whether tattoos are a good or a bad thing. Here is a part of Lisa's essay on reasons not to get tattoos:

"An elegant woman does not vandalize the temple she has been blessed with as her body. She appreciates it. She flaunts it. She's not happy with it? She goes to the gym. She dresses it up in lavish, fun, trendy clothes, enjoying trips to the mall with her girlfriends. She accentuates her legs with high heels. She gets her nails done. She enjoys the finer things in life, all with the body she was blessed with.

"But marking it up with ink? That's just not necessary."

Them's *not* fightin' words. However, a blogger in the tattoo community who caught the post wrote a vitriolic response to his community, creating an instant firestorm of criticism from his community aimed squarely at Lisa. Within two days, 23,000 people had clicked on her article (record traffic for the school newspaper). Soon there were 644 comments from around the world on Lisa's post. The response was overwhelmingly negative from the tight-knit tattoo community from Facebook to Reddit to Twitter and blogs.

Khoury wrote about the response:

"I woke up today and had 938 hate mails, 646 nasty Facebook comments, and dozens of mean-spirited tweets. In the past 48 hours, authors, war veterans, and mothers of small children have told me I'm ignorant, worthless, brainwashed, classless, disgusting, hypocritical, and judgmental."

She continued, "This column was meant to express my opinion and explain how I live, not to tell you that my way of life is in any way superior to yours.

"I was misinterpreted. These strangers have slowly and in the most painful way possible ripped me to shreds within the past 48 hours."

In an interview a short time after the incident, Lisa pointed out that the hate wasn't coming from her fellow students, her intended readers, but from small warrens of the Internet where narrow bands of zealotry thrive. She said, "There were professional journalists reaching out to me telling me to keep my head up. The people who mattered were supportive."

Almost two years after the firestorm, Lisa reflected on the experience with me. She was still astonished at the intensity of the vitriol aimed at a teenager who was brand new to journalism. The indelibleness of the Internet has been eye opening for her. She was still getting emails, both positive and negative, about the article. But the Internet doesn't distinguish between newcomers and veterans; the words are there for anyone to see, criticize, and share with others. She said, "I actually had a very positive experience after it happened. At first, I was devastated; the first few days I was so upset — people were calling me atrocious things. I had just started writing at my newspaper only a few months before. After I got over being so upset about it, I was just so fascinated by what had happened…I just felt this power — I can actually reach people with journalism. What if I can do that in a positive way? I got very interested in investigative journalism."

Fortunately for Khoury, she has the internal fortitude to withstand attacks from strangers. Indeed, she says she learned a valuable lesson about separating her true self from the target of the attacks. Her follow-up essay about her experience in the school newspaper was not only cathartic but well received by the campus community and other journalists. And a feature piece she wrote about how the school wasn't protecting students living off campus went viral and was picked up by CBS News and a few local news stations. She summed up her experience this way: "You get what you put into the Internet," she said, "Face-to-face engagement is always of primary importance, and the Internet is great for research and communicating with people, but it isn't life."

Online attacks can also form against an attacker.

The more passionate you are about a topic, the more likely it is that you can find a small space online where your fellow devotees gather. And in those spaces, passion can easily outstrip reason, common sense, and civility—and even a troll, a person used to heaping abuse on other people, can get trolled.

In 2012, Michael Brutsch was 49 years old and a former Air Force officer, a husband, an able programmer coding away at First Case Financial Services in Arlington, TX, father of a teenage son who had enlisted in the Marines, owner of seven cats and two dogs. It was a pretty normal life, he said. "I do my job, go home, watch TV, and go on the Internet."

At night, he and his wife had their laptops in bed, she posting photos of cute pictures of animals, while he posted child pornography and pictures of women being beaten. Brutsch's alter ego on Reddit was Violentacrez, a notorious Reddit organizer. Adrian Chen, who outed him on Gawker, wrote, "His specialty is distributing images of scantily clad underage girls, but, as Violentacrez, he also issued an unending fountain of racism, porn, gore, misogyny, incest, and exotic abominations yet unnamed, all on the sprawling online community Reddit."

Reddit gave him a ribald, robust, combative playground. In addition to all of the other roles he played in his life as a respectable employee and father, on Reddit, he was a joyful leader and distributor of filth as the voluntary moderator for four hundred subreddits, or conversational forums, with thousands of like-minded people. Brutsch said in his defense, "I just like riling people up in my spare time."

Riling people up is a wild understatement for one of the most renowned and reviled proponents of violence against women and child pornography in the wildest-west corner of the Internet. After being outed, Brutsch said,

"I got a home and a mortgage, and if this hits the fan, I believe this will affect negatively on my employment." Three days after he was outed, he was fired from his job.

To his comrades in child pornography and misogyny on Reddit, Brutsch is a hero, a part of their libertarian army devoted to free speech at any cost. Of course, many more people were appalled and repulsed by his behavior.

Surviving Online Mobs

Once online mobs form and become full throated, they are nearly impossible to stop. However, just because they are hard to stop doesn't mean that we should accept them as inevitable or not try to stop them. There is no way to stop information and stories from circulating, but there are ways to survive an Internet mob. As stated in Chapter One, we cannot *hope* for civility to blossom online — we need to *insist* on it.

The first thing we should all aim to do is to become as thoughtful as Lisa Khoury. Her defense mechanisms were spot on once she realized that none of the hoopla was real. It was one of those instances when online life was completely disconnected from on-land reality. The haters picked up one side of a point/counterpoint exchange and were off to the races in their own myopic unreasonableness that had absolutely nothing to do with Lisa as a real human being.

It is easy to get carried away online when we can't see and feel the personal harm we are doing. However, it is possible for those with built-in resilience to depersonalize it, as Lisa did, and recognize that the bullies don't actually know her — and that their opinions, therefore, don't define or harm her as a person. Easier said than done, of course, but still possible.

Philbert de Zwart wrote about Lisa's experience, "I really think that, in general, people have not lost this ability [to disagree civilly]...It's just that the people who have lost this ability are much more vocal and can distribute their bile at the click of a button. They don't realize and/or care that there is a human being at the other end and probably immediately go on with their lives with this annoyance off their chest."

The second lesson is aimed squarely at people like Judith Griggs and other leaders who have yet to learn how important it is to rehumanize themselves. A quick, heartfelt apology goes a long way toward squelching a fast-spreading brush fire. A good apology is not, "I'm sorry if you were offended by what I said" and definitely not Griggs' "You should be thanking me." A good apology is, "This is my fault; I'm sorry, and it is my responsibility to fix it." There should be a required class in college on sincere apologizing. The curriculum would include practice saying, "My fault," "I was wrong," "Thank you for pointing this out to me," and "Wow, I learned a lot from this." This class should replace the current class on CYA 101 with a final-exam essay chosen from the topics: "I'm sorry if you were offended by what I said," "I didn't realize you were so sensitive," or "We will look into whether this is offensive or not."

Although it may take some time for the reasonableness to be heard during a maelstrom, reasonable people will be there, a little quieter, perhaps, a little slow sometimes to voice their concerns, but they do arrive like the cavalry and ultimately calm everyone down.

The possibility of online eruptions isn't reason enough for withdrawal inside one's fortress walls. Organizations need to use the moment to engage in the conversation with the crowd, to explain their rationale for how they are working, and, most importantly, to ask for help to correct the problem. The organization is also obliged to follow up after a few weeks to report on promised progress and to continue to build Matterness with their crowd over time.

Conclusion

Action cascades are bigger, faster, and either more effective if done for positive reasons or more destructive when a mob forms, than any human efforts in the history of mankind. The management of action cascades takes intention and practice out loud and in public. Fear-based organizations are afraid of making public mistakes, which leaves them hoping for viral miracles rather than planning for action cascades. Even if something bad happens — misinformation takes hold, loud criticism erupts online, organizational leaders are attacked — it is no reason to withdraw. It should give a person or organization even greater reason to engage in conversation with the crowd and explain one's actions — even better, to ask for help to ensure the problem doesn't erupt again.

Discussion Questions

- Do we have the capacity to support a cascade? If thousands of people came knocking on our door today, do we have the server capacity needed to manage the conversations (or could we create it very quickly if budgetary issues are in play)? Other capacity issues include the ability to process large numbers of donations at a time and scale up inventory instantly.

- How could we turn an information cascade into an action cascade? What would people find most meaningful to do if a story we told became a cascade? (Note: The question isn't what *we* would like people to do but what *they* would like to do.)

Are we ready with the tools and channels to make these actions possible?

- What would we do if a mob formed? Are we already in communication with our crowds and building trust? Do we value transparency and welcome problem-solving help? Are we sincere when we apologize?

8 A Call for Collective Responsibility

MATTERNESS THRIVES IN environments that are flat and unfiltered. In these kinds of spaces, position and influence are ideally determined by performance and effort, rather than position and birthright. These characteristics should sound familiar as they are the same ones on which our American experiment in democracy are based. The United States was created as a society organized around individual achievement rather than inheritance. Anyone could become anything, we determined, through hard work. For most of our history, this meant that individual wealth and status were generated as one rose within institutional hierarchies.

The twentieth century was a triumph of man-made over natural forces. We became enthralled with automated, mechanized, artificial products and systems that pushed individuals to the sidelines. The dystopian vision of an America where robots took the place of humans increasingly became real as the century progressed. The only winners, the tip top of the income pyramid, were increasingly distanced and untouchable by the stresses and strains of life that most of us felt. We became separated from one another, pushed into our private, personal spaces, away from public ones. Our long-held assumptions about who we are and how we are different from every other country on earth were increasingly at odds with the reality of how we were living. Most people were left watching other people make decisions, get ahead, run for office, and shape public policies.

As in all other areas of society, social media shifted power from institutions to individuals in the civic arena, but not enough. The episodic bursts of democratic participation have been front-ended, such as voting, and fleeting, such as protests against racist police departments. It has not been enough to repair and rebalance society. These efforts are not making up for our collective loss of civic Matterness. We need to do more over time to change the dynamics between the governing and the governed.

Just as Matterness is paramount in our personal lives and our professional lives, it also needs to become a priority in our civic lives. As Peter Levine wrote in *We Are the Ones We've Been Waiting For* about the need for broad civic participation, "....deliberate and effective human action is one necessary condition of a worthwhile human life. If there is no agency, life is pointless."

We are at a distance from civic life, largely unaffiliated from political institutions, particularly political parties, government agencies (or if we are affiliated with them, it is likely to be for a bad reason, like incarceration or tax evasion), public commissions and committees. We need a different kind of civic life in order to regenerate civic Matterness. There are barriers to achieving a just and prosperous society that go beyond the organizational shortcomings previously addressed in this book. This chapter will address two of the most significant ones: the paucity of civic engagement and the privatization of our online public commons.

Civic Engagement. The most maddening parts of our current dysfunctional system — the avalanche of money in elections, the paralyzed policy making — are a direct result of the decline of Matterness between citizens and government. The intensively unsatisfying engagement with government that individuals have had at all levels over the last few decades has led most of us to withdraw from civic life, leaving the doing to professionals and narrow special-interest groups.

It is a mistake, though, to consider the lack of participation the same as disinterest. Americans care deeply and passionately about their communities, their children, and their economic futures.

The difference between anarchy and a civil society is the agreement of the citizenry to live within the agreed-upon rules. If we all woke up one morning and decided that we were going to run red lights, there wouldn't be enough cops on the planet to police us. But we don't — we have agreed to the most fundamental rules of society and are willing to live with the consequences of breaking them. We stop at red lights, pay for items in stores, and pay our taxes — at least enough of us to fund the government. Of course, there are times when laws simply don't work, like Prohibition, when enough people say that a law is silly or unjust or unenforceable, and then the law needs to change.

This makes us more than a society of laws; we are a society of norms that create agreed-upon ways of behaving civilly with one another. Norms are more important than laws because they create peer pressure for certain behaviors. For instance, there were no laws to protect gay people from hate crimes before there was a widespread belief that gay people deserved protection. When norms are established, politicians and policies follow; however, this happens to the benefit of the citizenry only when citizens are fully engaged in the process of creating policies and laws. We have the great fortune of living in a country where we can freely participate in civic life; we now need to choose to do so.

In the last decade, there have been episodic bursts of democracy activity centered on voter registration and voting. (Well, if you can vote, if your registration hasn't been expunged, if you can find your polling place, and if you have a lot of time to wait in lines and have the proper identification.) Even if we do vote, there is often no one to vote for. Unopposed elections for local and statewide elections are soaring. For instance, in Pennsylvania's 2010 election, 10 out of 25 state senators were unopposed and 95 out of 203 house races were also unopposed. Unopposed elected officials are accountable to no one. Unopposed majorities lead to patently undemocratic actions like gerrymandering election districts to ensure their continued majority status.

In addition to voting, the rise of social media has spearheaded a powerful, yet reactive, form of democratic participation. We've signed millions of online petitions, made moving videos, organized sit ins, boycotted products and identified potholes and parking meters to be fixed. These are all admirable actions, but they are also transactional, reactive, and fleeting. This is stop energy, and it isn't good enough to remake our economy and polity. We need to extend our engagement both earlier as policies are formed and later as the results begin to emerge. Citizens need to engage with government at all levels to create enough Matterness to allow for joint public problem solving.

Change.org, has realized the need to move from stop to go energy. It is the leading online petition site that has become extraordinarily successful as a platform for citizens to protest egregious practices and policies. However, as Jake Brewer, the Managing Director of External Affairs for the organization, said, "By having millions of people participating in a small democratic act of signing a petition, we created a lot of noise." Being yelled at by hundreds or thousands of millions of people is not a good way to encourage a policy maker or CEO to want to work with a crowd to change something. The site now enables the person or organization being petitioned to respond to the petitioners online and begin a dialogue about the situation. Brewer said, "Finding solutions that citizens weren't initially intending can be a better approach." It should not be surprising that direct conversations between people who are upset or affronted and the affronting party are powerful and constructive enough that it often undoes the need for the petition. Change.org is moving from a transactional approach to one centered on Matterness wherein people with a complaint are in direct conversation with people who can do something about the problem.

I discussed this issue with Noel Hidalgo, known widely and affectionately as No Neck, when he was the New York City coordinator for Code for America. Once a month, Noel organized a civic tech meeting in his offices. It was an opportunity for individual coders to meet one another in person to talk about how city government works. This is the civic education nobody receives in high school. Noel said that the volunteers were "deeply invested in how this city works." They didn't have political agendas as much as an interest in how the principles of access, transparency, and responsiveness can be incorporated into local government. Mostly, they spent their time wondering how government can be different and have a different relationship with the citizenry. Why is city government's default setting opaqueness rather than transparency? What do citizens want from their government? How can citizens work constructively with city government to produce apps and convert data sets into online, interactive maps? Noel also invited people from city agencies to discuss their work, their limitations, and the ways citizens can help. These back-and-forth conversations are where Matterness between government and citizens is being generated and grown.

Although organizations like Code for America are developing apps and other digital tools to make government more transparent and responsive to the citizenry, there is no magic app for how citizens can hold politicians and public policy makers accountable to their needs and interests. Rather, the growth of Matterness will happen through thousands of efforts to open up government decision-making and processes to the citizenry. In addition to focusing on Matterness as outlined in the previous chapters of this book, any effort to organize and galvanize citizen engagement with government agencies needs to include:

1. Significant Civic Education. There is an alarming lack of education on the part of citizens about government. Teaching civics and current events in schools is done poorly, with a focus on the recitation of facts and figures and little practical skills building to prepare children to participate in public life. Nancy Tate, Executive Director of the League of Women Voters, said, "No one is teaching individuals how to engage in the system." Organizations need to take the lead in teaching people how government works and how policy is made. We need to do much more than vote to create a more equitable society; we need to engage in the deliberate, long-term process of policy development. Where and how to begin to do that needs to be explained to people. Any advocacy organization, any company raising money for a significant public cause like breast cancer, needs to connect the dots for their constituents of how their money creates action somewhere that improves the lives of people. And any large-scale effort to improve the lives of citizens will inevitably involve governments. This is a fact whether people expect or want it to be true.

2. Organizations As Platforms. Time and again over the last decade, people have catalyzed social and political movements that organizations have then followed. There is a do-it-yourselfness to the way these efforts generally begin. The action cascades begin with a killing, a humiliation, a grievance so outrageous that others cannot turn away from it. The aggrieved party takes to social media to tell their story of injustice, a story that is moving and personal and easy for others to retell.

We understand the need to protest, to make our voices heard when we are aggrieved and an injustice has occurred. We are terrific at shouting from the mountain tops, signing petitions, making videos, and calling for resignations. The request for resolution is immediate and straightforward: arrest someone, change a rule, receive an apology. And therein lies the problem with do-it-yourself democracy; the resolutions are transactional rather than fundamental. People can be arrested, and even tried, companies can recall products, people can lose their jobs; however, the systems and policies that supported the original outrage are left in place. Citizens cannot do the heavy lifting of systems and policy change alone. They need organizations to fuel, support, and sustain these efforts over time.

Organizations focused on supporting citizen efforts cannot drive the agenda; instead, they must act like platforms. Platforms provide the scaffolding upon which educated, trained citizens can develop their own agendas and seek change. These platforms share information, provide training, make connections, sustain efforts during slow periods. This is what it means to work from the outside-in for these organizations, and, by doing so, they will develop a much broader base of support for any effort and create the kind of groundswell for policy change missing today.

3. Need for Both Volunteerism and Citizen Action. We became the most powerful country on earth not just because of our economic power but also because of our broad and deep participation in community life. We rolled up our sleeves and became the head of the program committee at the Elks Lodge, organized the annual fundraiser for the Rotary, manned the food pantry and cleaned up parks. Volunteerism for causes alone, though, cannot fix the deeply embedded problems that a dysfunctional government and political system are causing.

A recent USA TODAY/Bipartisan Policy Center poll found that twice as many people said that the way to make change in society is through volunteerism rather than being active in government. This dichotomous thinking causes millions of well-meaning people to serve soup to hungry people without addressing the underlying reasons why the richest nation on earth should have a significant portion of its citizenry chronically without food. It is the integration of volunteerism with public policy changes that will turn norms into policies.

Congress has a lower approval rating today than at any other time in the eighty-year history of Gallup polls. There is a great and growing chasm between what citizens care about (e.g., well-paying jobs) and what our public officials spend their time doing (e.g., fundraising). That is not a sustainable system. It may last for years, but, ultimately, a representative democracy has to represent the will of the people, or it becomes something else, an unrepresentative democracy, a theocracy or duopoly or oligarchy or any system weighted towards the interests of a few powerful actors that outweigh the interests, needs, desires, and thoughts of the people as a whole. We cannot abandon our government because it is dysfunctional; it is our job to fix it. At the same time, we cannot abandon citizens in need of housing, clothing, food, job training, health care and love. We need to do both of these jobs at the same time. We have the capacity to do both; we just need to be willing to do both.

Ultimately, our job is to participate in creating the society we want, not to watch others do so. This will only happen when citizens insist on having a real voice and input into policy making. Thomas Friedman wrote, "The standard answer [for increased citizen engagement] is that we need better leaders. The correct answer is that we need better citizens." Actually, we need both. We cannot ask citizens to engage in a system that isn't open to their involvement, and we cannot expect better leaders when citizens aren't involved to keep them accountable.

Taking Back the Commons.

Rebecca MacKinnon wrote in *Consent of the Networked*, "The digital commons is the virtual equivalent of Tocqueville's civil society, through which citizens can mobilize to express their interest and protect their rights."

The digital platforms we have been using to share, connect and organize ourselves over the past decade are not the open, public, places for sharing, connecting and organizing they appear to be. They look like the town commons; however, they are, in fact, private malls owned and operated by private companies more interested in profits than people.

There is a vast difference between bumping into an old friend on Main Street and hearing about a protest she started to force the town to do a better job of recycling, and not being able to see her post about this on Facebook because of the filter bubbles the company has created to serve their interests of selling more advertising. We are being intentionally kept from people and information online through the efforts of public companies acting like private guards.

It is enormously ironic that Silicon Valleyers who created platforms that professed to be everything that mainstream and broadcast media aren't have monetized their businesses in exactly the same way as traditional broadcast media — through soul-sucking ads and commercial intrusions. Creating and safeguarding an unfiltered commons is not their product, we are: Our attention, our awareness, our eyeballs, our interests, our wallets, our clicks. Jaron Lanier wrote, "There was a discernible ambient disgust with advertising in an earlier, more hippie-like phase of Silicon Valley, before the outlandish rise of Google." That's our bargain with these particular devils — we use their private sites as our public commons, and, in return, they commoditize us.

In their quest for generating Wall St.-pleasing profits, the platform providers are abusing Matterness by treating users as algorithms. As one Facebook user wrote, "I'm in my 20s, but they [Facebook] keep advertising retirement plans, old war movies on DVD, and, honest to God, dentures. You make ONE status update asking people to recommend a local dentist, and the Internet suddenly thinks you're a grizzled 80-year-old toothless war veteran."

Seventy-five percent of all email today is spam. Soon, a majority of the messages stuffed into our feeds will also be junk but harder to discern because of the intentional blurring of lines to make paid ads look like user-created information.

The concern isn't that social media platforms are becoming more like broadcast television; that is just disappointing. The concern is that most people using these platforms believe that they are open, safe spaces for public assembly that is guaranteed in our Constitution.

We need to insist that these private malls become more like public commons. We have to insist, at least, on the following conditions:

1. **Simple Terms of Agreement.** We deserve one-page terms of agreement in regular language, not in legal mumbo jumbo. Any longer, and we won't sign them. It shouldn't be a complicated arrangement if the intention is to use data only in pre-approved ways. The one page is simply the covenant between platform and user: "You are free to use our site, and, in return, we will use your data only in ways that you specifically give us permission for." How many lawyers would that take to draft?

2. **Option to Pay to Keep My Data Private.** Picking up and moving social networks can be enormously disruptive to the user — that is why AOL email addresses still exist. Rather than forcing users to look for new platforms, the platforms can provide unfiltered, ad-free spaces for a monthly fee. Spotify

is one company that has successfully created this kind of subscription service.

3. **Transparency.** The plans that public commons have to make money cannot be secret. Since the plans inevitably involve turning us into commodities, then we need to be allowed to weigh in on them. Companies will be surprised that, for the most part, people don't mind ads. What they mind are secrets. Of course, we realize that they need to make money; we deserve, though, the respect to be included in the discussion of exactly how they plan to make money off of our data. They may even be surprised by the interesting ideas we come up with!

Our charge at this moment is what it has always been; to insist on our right to be self-determining individuals, not anonymous drones in an enormous societal machinery. We must ensure that we are continuously building a society in which people's talents are allowed to shine and grievances can be heard without the prerequisite of position or money.

"Hope is belief in the plausibility of the possible, as opposed to the necessity of the probable," wrote Maimonides. We can create a collective future by insisting on what *could* happen rather than what we fear *must* happen.

Conclusion

For the last century, the dominant forms of organizing work were hierarchical structures whose purpose was to minimize risk and maximize control. These efforts, by definition, created criteria for who could get inside and how. At its most extreme, these bureaucracies became dehumanizing experiences and the stuff of ridicule by standup comics or horror stories by people caught inside an endless and maddening maze of forms and rules. These structures purposefully made workers and constituents matter less, to actually and purposefully dehumanize workers and constituents to ensure that work goes according to the plan of organizational leaders.

The last ten years has been a stunning shift in power from institutions to individuals across sectors and geography. What makes the lack of Matterness particularly piquant and painful now is that social media holds the promise that more people can have a voice and should be heard than ever before. For centuries, there was almost no recourse for people who felt abused or diminished by organizations. However, the last ten years has been an awakening of personal empowerment. And yet, creating a more equitable and prosperous society isn't being realized because leaders of organizations across sectors continue to work incredibly hard to maintain the illusion that they value their constituents while continuing to disempower them. Leaders are working in fearful ways at exactly the time when their organizations, constituents, and the world need them to be fearless.

There is much more work still to be done to ensure that the balance of the interest and needs between people and organizations becomes the norm, not the exception.

We need to succeed within a very stressful environment of technology, economic uncertainty, and social unrest, but that shouldn't stop us. There are significant choices each one of us can make to lead fearlessly and position ourselves to matter more inside and outside of organizations.

Take a Deep Breath. People are using social media to express themselves, start businesses, access information and services, organize, and protest. Each one of us can know more, see more, and share more today. We are also more overwhelmed and more distracted than ever before. But within the swirl of all of the technological newness, all of the information available to us and coming at us, all of the messages demanding our attention and response, we are still what we've always been — social, hard working, generous, only out loud, in real time, and for the world to see. Our best selves are most often shining through.

Even so, our always-on technology can easily feel overwhelming, unmanageable, and not sustainable. It's exacerbated by the exuberance and breathlessness over analysis with which each new tool is greeted. Email and blogs were supplanted in the popular imagination as Facebook, Twitter, and YouTube became the hot new channels, which themselves have now been replaced at the cafeteria table reserved for the cool kids by Snapchat and Whatsapp. And these tools will be replaced by something else with a funny name in another month or two. The focus on each tool, which fundamentally does the same thing as the last one by connecting people to one another and enabling the easy and wide sharing of digital information, makes the disruption seem more chaotic than necessary.

We need to turn off the constantly beeping and pinging sounds from our gadgets that distract us from whatever else we were thinking of doing. We need to regularly shut down and recharge in order to maintain our health and our creativity. As outlined in Chapter Four, organizations that are insisting that their employees shut down — Menlo software in Minneapolis, Volkswagen in Germany — are more productive and more profitable, and keep their employees longer. Choosing to shut off the technology is not the same as being uncompetitive. Multi-tasking is an unproductive way to work and live — as parents frantically return emails during their children's soccer games, neither working nor watching well. Leaders can insist that after work is the time to shut down, not the time to keep working ourselves into exhausted heaps of humanity.

It is a *choice* to be always on, but it is a better *choice* to shut down occasionally and become more productive and happier people.

Organizations Need to Embrace Matterness. Organizations that are using social media to feign engagement *with* constituents while continuing to work *at* people through press releases and advertisements are doing more harm than good to themselves and their constituents. Fear-driven organizations view the world as more frightening and dangerous than it really is, creating counterproductive and ultimately unsuccessful efforts to try to control uncontrollable people and events.

Organizations need to become more purposeful about engaging with the world and spend less time on The Churn-feeding concerns about what could go wrong rather than what could go right. It takes intentional effort to reverse the now regular slide into anti-Matterness, to quiet all of the internal noise, to intentionally take down the high walls that separate them from their own supporters and withstand the pressure to spend every minute of the day checking things off the ever-growing to-do list. However, just because it is difficult doesn't mean it isn't possible or important to do.

Learning how to be in conversation with staff and constituents is an empowering way of being that changes the nature of work from endless and reactive to-do lists to powerful ways to engage people to become problem solvers and ambassadors for the organization.

Relationships Matter Most. When my nephew was young he struggled to decide whether food or football was the most important thing in his life. It was a difficult choice. But, in the realm of people and organizations, in the space where they each need to matter and be heard, relationships matter the most. People are beautiful mosaics of flaws and strengths, and it is disingenuous and exhausting to pretend differently. This is one of the drivers of The Churn, the enormous energy spent pretending that people are all the same and mistake-free. Of course, things go wrong, a staff person is rude, the store opened late, a donor wasn't thanked, our show didn't sell out. Things go wrong every day, but almost all of them are unimportant, small things. We need to focus on people inside and outside of organizations sincerely trying to build great products, right societal wrongs, and provide services. Listening to each other's stories, trying to understand why they are upset, being in conversation rather than yelling at one another are the only ways to understand why people are doing what they're doing.

Insist on Civility. We are not predetermined to be rude, greedy, insensitive, or selfish. We need to insist that our best selves, the ones filled with generosity, kindness, and empathy, are expected to supersede our most frightened and stressed ones. We need to insist on civility both on land and online at all times. We need to collectively and actively promote and celebrate acts of civility, as well as quickly condemn acts of incivility and the platform providers that, at times, enable them. This isn't a choice but a necessity for creating a civil society that meets the needs of most of its citizenry.

We are neither helpless, nor should we feel hopeless, in our pursuit of productive, profitable, meaningful private and professional lives. We can choose to manage our gadgets rather than be managed by them. We must insist on greater civility online and on land, or we can capitulate to vulgarity and bullying. Most of all, we can demand that we matter as individuals, that our opinions and skills deserve to be heard and appreciated, and push back against institutional forces that want to commoditize us.

Acknowledgments

WRITING ANY BOOK REQUIRES the writer to be a master at self-delusion. The delusion begins with the assumption that, each time a book is written, it will be easier than the last — it isn't. The delusion continues with the assumption that what one writes will make sense to anyone else. It rarely does, in my experience, until at least the thirty-seventh version. And finally, the delusion's third act is the assumption that someone, anyone really, out there will be interested in what has been written. Of course, only you, the reader, can determine whether this last delusion is true. The only thing that stands between these delusions and despair is a small group of hardy people who have steadfastly supported this endeavor in just the right time and manner throughout the process.

I am grateful and indebted to Debra Askanase, who read every nonsensical proposal and maddeningly elliptical chapter with unfailing grace. Debra, thank you so much for your steadfast support and smart insights. My thanks also to Lisa Colton, Kate Lauzar, and Tom

Watson for slogging through bad drafts and providing great feedback.

The idea for *Matterness* crystalized during a meeting organized by Adina Frydman of the Synergy program at the UJA-Federation of New York. I am enormously grateful to Adina for her constant support, wisdom, and calmness over the last few years and hope she continues to so selflessly help me in the future.

Nils Parker is an exceptionally talented editor in addition to being unshakably wise, calm, and thoughtful — all enviable talents and characteristics. Thanks to Michele DeFilippo, Ronda Rawlins, and their colleagues at 1106 Design, LLC for their incredible array of excellent services. Julie Trelstad, one of the country's leading experts on independent publishing, answered all of my questions with unending patience and good cheer.

I owe a special thanks to the people who shared their time and stories with me. Mark Horvath, Michael Wood-Lewis, Harry Geyser, Jennifer James, Megan Kashner, Elissa Edgerton Black, Noel Hildalgo, Lisa Khoury, David Bley, Kronda Adair, and Dan Savage. Their heroic efforts to incorporate Matterness into their work and lives is inspiring. Thanks to my friend Henry Timms, who is one of the most innovative thinkers around today. Henry leads by example with grace and humility every day. And, a very special thanks to my dear friend, Lisa Belkin, for her help, guidance, and support — and for our many lunches, past, present, and future.

This book is a continuation of the thinking and writings of many other people. These thinkers, authors, and doers include Micah Sifry, Clay Shirky, Adam Grant, Susan Cain, Douglas Rushkoff, Jaron Lanier, Eric Ries, Daniel H. Pink, Doc Searls, Chip and Dan Heath, Peter Levine, and Brigid Schulte. In addition, I want to thank Beth Kanter for her ongoing leadership and support of my work over the past ten years of our very interesting journey together. I sincerely hope I have done justice to their ideas and thoughts.

And finally, of course, my sincere thanks and eternal gratitude to all of my boys, big and small, for their ongoing and everlasting love, patience, and support.

Notes

Introduction

1. Rob Schmitz, "Former Homeless Man's Videos Profiles Life on the Street," NPR, Weekend Edition Saturday, posted on March 6, 2010, http://www.npr.org/templates/story/story.php?storyId=124356908, accessed on May 12, 2013.
2. Mark Horvath, interview with Allison Fine, Social Good Podcast, posted on February 13, 2012, accessed on May 12, 2013.
3. Mark Horvath, "Why Do We Kick Homeless People Out of Winter Shelter in Bad Weather?" posted on December 20, 2010, http://www.huffingtonpost.com/mark-horvath/homeless-winter-shelter_b_798932.html, accessed on February 13, 2012.
4. Mark Horvath, "The Power of Social Media Helping Homeless Services After Hurricane Katrina," posted on November 2, 2012, http://www.huffingtonpost.com/mark-horvath/power-of-social-media-hel_b_2062290.html, accessed on May 12, 2013.

5. Beth Kanter and Allison Fine, *The Networked Nonprofit*, Jossey-Bass, John Wiley & Sons, 2010.
6. John Goodman, Manage Complaints to Enhance Loyalty, Association of Quality Progress, February 2006, http://www.texas-quality.org/SiteImages/125/Reference%20Library/Manage%20Complaints%20to%20Enhance%20Loyalty.pdf, accessed on August 14, 2014.
7. Here's What Happens When You Don't Listen to Your Customers Complaints, Ira Kalb, Marshall School of Business, Business Insider, posted on January 19, 2012, http://www.businessinsider.com/heres-what-happens-when-you-dont-listen-to-your-customers-complaints-2012-1, accessed on August 12, 2014.
8. Mabel Birungi Komunda, "Customer Complaints Behavior, Service Recovery and Behavioral Intentions: Literature Review," *International Journal of Business and Behavioral Sciences*, Vol. 3, No. 7, July 2013, http://cprenet.com/uploads/archive/IJBBS_12-1177.pdf, accessed on November 1, 2013.
9. Ritu Sharma, "How Nonprofits Use Social Media to Engage With Their Communities," *Nonprofit Quarterly*, posted on March 13, 2014, https://nonprofitquarterly.org/management/23837-how-nonprofits-use-social-media-to-engage-with-their-communities.html, accessed on May 12, 2014.
10. Martiz Research and evolve24 Twitter Study, September 2011, http://www.maritzresearch.com/~/media/Files/MaritzResearch/e24/ExecutiveSummaryTwitterPoll.ashx, accessed on August 12, 2014.
11. "Congress and the Public," Gallup Poll, posted on August 1, 2014, http://www.gallup.com/poll/1600/congress-public.aspx, accessed on September 2, 2014.

12. 2014 Edelman Trust Barometer, http://www.edelman.com/insights/intellectual-property/2014-edelman-trust-barometer/, accessed on July 3, 2014.
13. David Callahan, J. Mijin Cha, "Stacked Deck" Demos: A Network of Ideas and Action, http://www.demos.org/stacked-deck-how-dominance-politics-affluent-business-undermines-economic-mobility-america, February 29, 2013, http://www.demos.org/stacked-deck-how-dominance-politics-affluent-business-undermines-economic-mobility-america, accessed on June 5, 2013.
14. Micah Sifry, "The Big Disconnect," unpublished manuscript, page 27.
15. Archbishop of Boston...Tweet from Rhona Fischman on Nov. 13, 2013

Chapter One: Tyranny of Dichotomy

1. Ray Robinson, "Baseball: A Bad Guy Who Finished First," *New York Times*, published April 4, 2003, http://www.nytimes.com/1993/04/04/books/baseball-a-bad-guy-who-finished-first.html, accessed on July 18, 2014.
2. Kate Shaw, "Stone Age Social Networks May Have Resembled Ours," *Ars Technica Wired* Magazine, http://www.wired.com/2012/01/stone-age-social-networking/, posted on January 27, 2010, http://www.wired.com/2012/01/stone-age-social-networking/, accessed on February 21, 2014.
3. Definition of homophily from Nicholas A. Christakis and James H. Fowler, *Connected: The Suprising Power of Our Social Networks and How They Shape Our Lives*, Little, Brown and Company, 2009, page 17.

4. Layous K, Nelson SK, Oberle E, Schonert-Reichl KA, Lyubomirsky S (2012) "Kindness Counts: Prompting Prosocial Behavior in Preadolescents Boosts Peer Acceptance and Well-Being." PLoS ONE 7(12): e51380. doi:10.1371/journal.pone.0051380, accessed online on September 27, 2013.
5. Daniel Stimson, "Inner Workings of the Magnanimous Mind," News from NINDS, posted on April 7, 2004, http://www.ninds.nih.gov/news_and_events/news_articles/brain_activity_during_altruism.htm, accessed on September 27, 2013.
6. The Center on Philanthropy at Indiana University, Giving USA 2012, Executive Summary, http://store.givingusareports.org/Giving-USA-2012-The-Annual-Report-on-Philanthropy-for-the-Year-2011-Executive-Summary-P43.aspx, downloaded on November 8, 2013, page 8.
7. Tamas Bereczkei, Bela Birkas, Zsuzsanna Kerekes, "Altruism Towards Strangers in Need: Costly Signaling in an Industrial Society," *Evolution and Human Behavior* 31 (2010) 95–103, posted on July 18, 2009. http://www.evolutionpsychology.com/uploads/9/3/4/5/9345921/altruism_towards_strangers_in_need_ehb2010.pdf, page 97, accessed on November 11, 2013.
8. Molly McLure Wasko and Samer Faraj, "Why Should I Share? Examining Social Capital and Knowledge Contribution in Electronic Networks of Practice," *MIS Quarterly*, 2005, http://misq.org/why-should-i-share-examining-social-capital-and-knowledge-contribution-in-electronic-networks-of-practice.html, accessed on October 23, 2013.
9. "Homocide Trends in the United States, 1980–2008, annual Rates for 2009, 2010." NCJ 236018, U.S. Department of Justice, Office of Justice Programs, Bureau of Justice Statistics, posted on November 2011,

http://www.bjs.gov/content/pub/pdf/htus8008.pdf, accessed on October 12, 2013.

10. National statistics for violent crimes by state and city are maintained by the FBI at http://www.fbi.gov/about-us/cjis/ucr/ucr.
11. Simone Roberts, Jijun Zhang, Jennifer Truman, Thomas D. Snyder, "Indicators of School Crime and Violence: 2010," U.S. Department of Education, National Center for Educational Statistics, NCES 2011-002, Bureau of Justice Statistics, U.S. Department of Education, U.S. Department of Justice Office of Justice Programs, NCJ 230812, November 2010, http://nces.ed.gov/pubs2011/2011002.pdf, accessed on August 12, 2013.
12. Emmanuel Saez, "Striking it Richer: The Evolution of the Top Incomes in the United States" (Updated with 2012 preliminary estimates), http://elsa.berkeley.edu/~saez/saez-UStopincomes-2012.pdf, UC Berkeley, September 3, 2013, accessed on March 12, 2014. University of California, Department of Economics, 530 Evans Hall #3880, Berkeley, CA 94720. This is an updated version of "Striking It Richer: The Evolution of Top Incomes in the United States," *Pathways* Magazine, Stanford Center for the Study of Poverty and Inequality, Winter 2008, 6–7.
13. Kevin Roose, "The Commuter Kings: Riding Along on Silicon Valley's Exclusive Shuttles," posted on December 26, 2012, http://nymag.com/daily/intelligencer/2012/12/silicon-valleys-exclusive-shuttles.html), accessed March 24, 2014.
14. Neli Esipova, Anita Pugliese, and Julie Ray, "381 Million Adults Worldwide Migrate Within Countries, U.S. One of the Most Mobile Countries in the World, *Gallup World*, May 15, 2013, http://www.gallup.com/poll/162488/381-million-adults-worldwide-migrate-

within-countries.aspx?utm_source=alert&utm_medium=email&utm_campaign=syndication&utm_content=morelink&utm_term=All%20Gallup%20 Headlines, accessed on February 12, 2014.

15. David K. Ihrke and Carole S. Faber, "Geographical Mobility: Population Characteristics," U.S. Department of Commerce, Economics and Statistics Administration, U.S. Census Bureau, issued December 2012, http://www.census.gov/prod/2012pubs/p20-567.pdf, P20-567, accessed February 13, 2014.
16. Tamar Lewin, "Record Number Complete High School and College," *The New York Times,* November 5, 2012, http://www.nytimes.com/2012/11/06/education/record-numbers-of-young-americans-earn-bachelors-degree.html?_r=2&, accessed February 3, 2014.
17. Heather Kelly, "YouTube Tries to Fix Its Comments," CNN Tech, Posted on September 24, 2013, http://www.cnn.com/2013/09/24/tech/social-media/youtube-comment-upgrade/, accessed on November 15, 2013.

Chapter Two: Big Small Towns

1. State and County Quickfacts, United States Census Bureau, http://quickfacts.census.gov/qfd/states/36/3667638.htmlm accessed January 21, 2014 for information on Sleepy Hollow, NY.
2. Wellman, B., and M. Gulia. 1999. Net-surfers don't ride alone: Virtual communities as communities. In Networks in the Global Village: Life in Contemporary Communities, ed. B. Wellman, page 331–66.
3. Howard Rheingold, *Virtual Communities,* MIT Press, 1993, page 5.
4. Wenhong Chen, Jeffrey Boase, Barry Wellman, "The Global Villagers: Comparing Internet Users

and Uses Around the World," http://www.ryerson.ca/~jboase/assets/chen-boase-and-wellman-2002-the-global-villagers.pdf, Pp. 74–113 in *The Internet in Everyday Life*, edited by Barry Wellman and Caroline Haythornthwaite, accessed on October 12, 2013.

5. Samuel M. Wilson and Leighton C. Peterson, "The Anthropology of Online Communities," *Annual Review of Anthropology*, Vol. 31: 449–467 (Volume publication date October 2002), First published online as a Review in Advance on June 14, 2002, DOI: 10.1146/annurev.anthro.31.040402.085436, accessed on November 15, 2013.
6. Alice Marwick, interview with Allison Fine, June 1, 2013.
7. Tim Simonite, "What Facebook Knows," June 13, 2012, *MIT Review*, http://www.technologyreview.com/featuredstory/428150/what-facebook-knows/, accessed on December 4, 2013.
8. Moira Burke, Cameron Marlow, Thomas Lento, "Social Network Activity and Social Well-Being," published June 8, 2011, accessed February 12, 2014. http://www.scribd.com/doc/57223242/Social-Network-Activity-and-Social-Well-Being,
9. Author's visit to and interview of Michael Wood-Lewis and users of Front Porch Forum in Burlington, VT, on July 25, 2013.
10. Stuart Comstock-Gay, interview with Allison Fine, July 26, 2013.
11. Jennifer James, interview with Allison Fine, February 28, 2014.
12. Jennifer James, interview with Allison Fine for Social Good Podcast, posted on May 9, 2013, http://philanthropy.com/article/Unleashing-the-Power-of/138891/ accessed on March 1, 2014.

13. Tom Watson, "Mom Bloggers Build a Network for Activism and Change," posted on May 12, 2013, http://www.forbes.com/sites/tomwatson/2013/05/12/mom-bloggers-build-a-network-for-activism-and-change/, accessed on March 11, 2014.
14. Jennifer James, "Technology and Global Change: From Conversation to Action," Bill and Melinda Gates Foundation, posted on January 15, 2014,
15. http://www.impatientoptimists.org/Posts/2014/01/Global-Conversations-Today-and-Tomorrow, accessed on March 2, 2014.
16. Jennifer Barbour, interview with Allison Fine, March 6, 2014.
17. Jennifer Barbour, "Philanthropy Friday: Generosity Has No Language," Another Jennifer Blog + Writing Lab, March 21, 2014, http://anotherjennifer.com/philanthropy-friday-generosity-has-no-language-barrier/, accessed on March 22, 2014.
18. Sharon Jayson, "Internet Leads to Dates and Relationships," *USA Today*, posted on October 21, 2013, http://www.usatoday.com/story/news/nation/2013/10/21/dating-online-mobile-pew/2995323/, accessed on February 11, 2014.
19. Ruth Sykes interview with Allison Fine, November 1, 2013.
20. Madeleine Taylor interview with Allison Fine, October 10, 2013.
21. Adam Grant, "Finding the Hidden Value in Your Network," posted on June 17, 2013, LinkedIn, http://www.linkedin.com/today/post/article/20130617112202-69244073-finding-the-hidden-value-in-your-network, accessed on September 24, 2013.
22. Mark S. Granovetter, "The Strength of Weak Ties," *American Journal of Sociology*, Volume 78, Issue 6 (May 1973)

23. Tim Simonite, "What Facebook Knows," June 13, 2012, *MIT Review*, http://www.technologyreview.com/featuredstory/428150/what-facebook-knows/, accessed on December 4, 2013. *"It is our diverse collection of weak ties that most powerfully determines what information we're exposed to."*
24. Daniel Z. Levin, Jorge Walter, J. Keith Murnighan, "The Power of Reconnection — How Dormant Ties Can Surprise You," *MIT Sloan Management Review*, posted on March 23, 2011, http://sloanreview.mit.edu/article/the-power-of-reconnection-how-dormant-ties-can-surprise-you/, accessed on February 12, 2014.
25. Susan Cain, *Quiet*, Crown Publishing Group, 2012, page 63.
26. Allison Fine, Network Builders session at the Case Foundation, private notes, June, 2010.
27. Matthew W. Brault, "Americans with Disabilities: 2010," Household Economic Studies, Current Population Reports, U.S. Census Bureau, Issued July 2012, http://www.census.gov/prod/2012pubs/p70-131.pdf, accessed February 12, 2014.
28. Emma Tracey, "Social Networking, the Disabled View," BBC News, posted on April 5, 2011, http://www.bbc.co.uk/ouch/features/social_network_savvie.shtml, accessed on January 23, 2014.
29. Thomas C. Weiss, "Persons with Disabilities and Entrepreneurship," *Disabled World*, posted on July 4, 2009 (revised June 24, 2010), http://www.disabled-world.com/editorials/disablity-entrepreneurship-tips.php, accessed March 21, 2014.
30. Aaron Smith, "How Americans Use Text Messaging," Pew Research Internet Project, posted on September 19, 2011, http://www.pewinternet.org/2011/09/19/how-americans-use-text-messaging/, accessed on January 12, 2014.

31. Arnold Samlan, "Reclaiming My Social Media," JewPoint, Darim Online, posted on May 22, 2014, http://darimonline.org/blog/reclaiming-my-social-media, accessed on May 23, 2014.

Chapter Three: Working From the Inside Out

1. Richard Sandomir, "U.S.T.A. Sues Filmmakers of 'Venus and Serena'," *The New York Times*, posted on June 17, 2013, http://straightsets.blogs.nytimes.com/2013/06/17/u-s-t-a-sues-filmmakers-of-venus-and-serena-documentary/?_php=true&_type=blogs&_r=0, accessed on November 15, 2013.
2. Carolyn Heller Baird, Gautaum Paranis, "From Social Media to Social CRM, IBM Institute for Business Value," IBM Global Business Services, Executive Report, posted on Slideshare on April 15, 2011, http://www.slideshare.net/IBMDK/from-social-media-to-social-crm-ibm-insitute-for-business-value, accessed November 16, 2013. Chart is on page 9.
3. Chip Heath, Dan Heath, *Made to Stick: Why Some Ideas Survive and Others Die*, New York, Random House, 2007, pages 19-20.
4. Mabel Birungi Komunda, "Customer Complaints Behavior, Service Recovery and Behavioral Intentions: Literature Review," *International Journal of Business and Behavioral Sciences*, Vol. 3, No. 7, July 2013, accessed on November 1, 2013.
5. Ozlem Atalik. (2007). "Customer Complaints About Airline Service: A Preliminary Study of Turkish Frequent Flyers," *Management Research News*, 30, 6, 409-419, 2007.
6. Stephen S. Tax, Stephen W. Brown, "Recovering and Learning from Service Failure," *MIT Sloan Management Review*, Fall 1998, posted on October 15,

1998, http://sloanreview.mit.edu/article/recovering-and-learning-from-service-failure/, accessed on October 1, 2013.

7. James G. Maxham III, Richard G. Netemeyer, "Modeling Customer Perceptions of Complaint Handling Over Time: The Effects of Perceived Justice on Satisfaction and Intent," *Journal of Retailing*, published in 2002 by New York University, http://www.fdewb.unimaas.nl/meteor/eden/Mike%20Brady/Maxham%20and%20Netemeyer.pdf, accessed on November 1, 2013.
8. Michael A. McCollough, Leonard L. Berry, Manjit S. Yadav, "An Empirical Investigation of Customer Satisfaction After Service Failure and Recovery," *Journal of Service Research* 2000; 3; 121, Sage Publications, http://jsr.sagepub.com/content/3/2/121.abstract.
9. Tony Schwartz, Christine Porath, "Why You Hate Work," *The New York Times* Sunday Review, posted on May 30, 2014, http://www.nytimes.com/2014/06/01/opinion/sunday/why-you-hate-work.html?_r=2&utm_content=buffer8e2b4&utm_medium=social&utm_source=twitter.com&utm_campaign=buffe, accessed on June 5, 2014.
10. Richard C. Harwood, John A. Creighton, "The Organization-First Approach," Harwood Institute for Public Innovation, February 2009, http://www.theharwoodinstitute.org/wp-content/uploads/2012/07/The_Organization_First_Report.pdf, accessed on October 14, 2013.
11. Matt Flegenheimer, "Report Finds Punctuality Trumps Safety at Metro-North," *New York Times*, March 14, 2014, http://www.nytimes.com/2014/03/14/nyregion/safety-is-lacking-at-metro-north-us-review-finds-after-a-fatal-crash.html, accessed on April 20, 2014.

12. Aaron Smith, "How Americans Use Text Messaging," Pew Research Internet Project, posted on September 19, 2011, http://www.pewinternet.org/2011/09/19/how-americans-use-text-messaging/, accessed on January 12, 2014.
13. Eyal Olphir, Clifford Nass and Anthony D. Wagner, "Cognitive Control in Media Multitaskers," vol. 106 no. 37, Proceedings of the National Academy of Sciences of the United States of America, approved on July 20, 2009, http://www.pnas.org/content/106/37/15583.long, accessed on December 21, 2014.
14. "The Effects of Multitasking on Organizations," Realization, http://www.realization.com/pdf/Effects_of_Multitasking_on_Organizations.pdf, accessed on June 12, 2014.
15. Alice Marwick, "Status Update: Celebrity, Publicity, and Self-Branding in Web 2.0," Dissertation, New York University, 2010, page 18.

Chapter Four: Leading From the Outside In

1. Sam Roudman, "How Open Source Civic Technology Helped Flu Vaccinations Go Viral," TechPresident, posted on January 15, 2013, http://techpresident.com/news/23371/flu-vaccination-app-goes-viral-civic-hackers, accessed on February 5, 2014.
2. Henry Timms, interview with Allison Fine, March 4, 2014.
3. Tom Ley, "How Did Roger Goodell's Twitter Chat Go? Not So Well!" Deadspin, posted on May 6, 2014, http://deadspin.com/how-did-roger-goodells-twitter-chat-go-not-so-well-1572557823, accessed on May 20, 2014.
4. David Bley, interview with Allison Fine, March 10, 2014.

5. Sara Radicati, "Email Statistics Report, 2011-2015," posted on April 14, 2014, http://www.radicati.com/wp/wp-content/uploads/2014/04/Email-Statistics-Report-2014-2018-Executive-Summary.pdf, accessed on June 5, 2014.
6. Brigid Schulte, *Overwhelmed: Work, Love and Play When No One Has the Time*, Sarah Chrichton Books, 2014, page 145–147.
7. *Ibid.*, page 125.
8. Author email with Carsten Krebs, Director of Corporate Communications, Volkswagen Group of America, June 3, 2014.
9. Sarah Kliff, "Why Komen Defunded Planned Parenthood," *Washington Post*, posted on January 28, 2012, accessed on May 5, 2014.
10. Mrinal Desai, "Successful Word of Mouth Marketing," Creative Brand Communications website, posted on May 23, 2008, http://www.creative-brand.com/branding/successful-word-of-mouth-marketing, accessed on June 16, 2014.
11. Boris Groysberg, Michael Slind, "Leadership Is a Conversation," June 2012, http://hbr.org/2012/06/leadership-is-a-conversation/ar/1, accessed on September 12, 2013.
12. *Oxford English Dictionary*, http://www.oxforddictionaries.com/us/definition/american_english/natural-language, accessed on May 15, 2014.

Chapter Five: Scaling Matterness Within Organizations

1. Alicia Ciccone, "The True Cost of Hiring Employees," HuffPost News and Trends, posted on June 4, 2012, http://www.huffingtonpost.com/2012/06/04/

the-true-cost-of-hiring-infographic_n_1568295.html, accessed on October 13, 2013.

2. Adarsh Kumar Kakar, "What Motivates Team Members and Users of Agile Projects?" Proceedings of the Southern Association for Information Systems Conference, Savannah GA, US, March 8–9, 2013, http://sais.aisnet.org/2013/Kakar2.pdf, accessed on October 21, 2013.
3. Doctrine for the Armed Forces of the United States, March 25, 2013, http://www.dtic.mil/doctrine/new_pubs/jp1.pdf, page I-1, accessed on July 12, 2014.
4. Ken Segall, *Insanely Simple*: The Obsession That Drives Apple's Success, Portfolio/Penguin, 2012, page 8.
5. The Container Store, "Our Foundation Principles," http://standfor.containerstore.com/our-foundation-principles/, accessed on March 12, 2014.
6. "100 Best Companies to Work For," *Fortune* Magazine, http://archive.fortune.com/magazines/fortune/best-companies/2014/list/?iid=BC14_sp_full, accessed on March 12, 2014.
7. Maria Nicanor, "Endings and Beginnings," Guggenheim Lab Log, posted on January 29, 2014, http://blogs.guggenheim.org/lablog/endings-beginnings/, accessed on February 15, 2014.
8. Elissa Black Edgerton, interview with Allison Fine, April 28, 2014.
9. Leah Neaderthal, "You Have to Start Somewhere: 4 Steps to Eliminating Decision Paralysis," Lean Impact: Lean for Social Good, posted on April 30, 2013, http://www.leanimpact.org/4-steps-to-eliminating-decision-paralysis/#sthash.5K4g2fJp.dpuf, accessed on Juily 21, 2014.
10. Eli Pariser, *The Filter Bubble*, The Penguin Press, 2011, page 3.

11. Paul J.H. Schoemaker, Steve Krupp, and Samantha Howland, "Strategic Leadership: The Essential Skills," *Harvard Business Review*, January-February 2013, http://hbr.org/2013/01/strategic-leadership-the-esssential-skills/ar/3, accessed on July 15, 2014.
12. John Koetsier, "Breaking: Adria Richards Fired by SendGrid for Calling Out Developers on Twitter," *VB News*, posted on March 21, 2013, updated on March 22, 2013, http://venturebeat.com/2013/03/21/breaking-adria-richards-fired-by-sendgrid-for-outting-developers-on-twitter/, accessed on January 15, 2014.
13. Andy Vuong, "SendGrid Fires Adria Richards After Online Firestorm Over Inappropriate Jokes," *The Denver Post*, Techknow Bytes, posted on March 21, 2013, http://blogs.denverpost.com/techknow bytes/2013/03/21/boulder-based-sendgrid-fires-employee-after-firestorm-over-jokes/9367/, accessed on January 15, 2014.
14. Mr-Hank comment on Hacker News, posted on March 19, 2013, https://news.ycombinator.com/item?id=5398681, accessed on January 15, 2014.
15. Michal Kohane, "40 Plus and Screwed: More on Less Young Adult Engagement," eJewish Philanthropy, posted on June 19, 2013, http://ejewishphilanthropy.com/40-plus-and-screwed-more-on-less-young-adult-engagement/, accessed on January 15, 2014.

Chapter Six: Working With Crowds to Scale Matterness

1. Jon L. Pierce, Stephen A. Rubenfield, Susan Morgan, "Employee Ownership: A Conceptual Model of Process and Effects," *The Academy of Management Review*, Vol. 16, No. 1 (January 1991), page 121-144.

2. Wikipedia page, Dove Campaign for Real Beauty, http://en.wikipedia.org/wiki/Dove_Campaign_for_Real_Beauty, accessed on October 21, 2013.
3. YouTube, "Dove Real Beauty Sketches, posted on April 14, 2013, http://www.youtube.com/watch?v=XpaOjMXyJGk, accessed on October 21, 2013.
4. Laura Stampler, "Why People Hate Dove's 'Real Beauty Sketches' Video," *Business Insider*, posted on April 22, 2013, http://www.businessinsider.com/why-people-hate-doves-real-beauty-ad-2013-4, accessed on October 21, 2013.
5. Jack Neff, "Dove: The Evolution from 'Evolution'," *Advertising Age*, posted on June 11, 2013, http://adage.com/article/news/dove-evolution-evolution/241971/, accessed on October 21, 2013.
6. Joel Benenson, Benenson Strategy Group, Jan van Lohuizen, Voter Consumer Research, "The Rapid Increase in Support for Marriage Changes Political Equation: Emerging Majority Supports the Freedom to Marry," written July 27, 2011, http://freemarry.3cdn.net/5ae85613318ade1b2e_8dm6bnq72.pdf, accessed on August 23, 2014.
7. Zach Wahls, Iowa Student, Pro Gay Marriage Speech Goes Viral Again, Huffington Post, December 1, 2011, http://www.huffingtonpost.com/2011/12/01/zach-wahls-iowa-student-marriage-equality_n_1123020.html, accessed on May 5, 2014.
8. Kickstarter Stats, https://www.kickstarter.com/help/stats, accessed on July 23, 2014.
9. Ruth Simon, "Banks Reach Out to Small Firms," *Wall Street Journal*, posted on February 8, 2011, http://online.wsj.com/news/articles/SB10001424052748703507804576130591215860046, accessed on October 22, 2013.

10. Panel presentation by Liezl Van Riper on, "Tapping the Crowd to Solve Social Inequity," for Emerging Practitioners in Philanthropy, posted on January 29, 2014, http://www.epip.org/2014/01/event-recap-tapping-the-crowd-to-solve-social-inequity/, accessed on March 2, 2014.
11. Suw Charman-Anderson, "Kickstarter: Dream Maker or Promise Breaker?," *Forbes*, posted on November 30, 2012, http://www.forbes.com/sites/suwcharmananderson/2012/11/30/kickstarter-dream-maker-or-promise-breaker/, accessed on May 5, 2014.
12. Ethan R. Mollick, "The Dynamics of Crowdfunding: An Exploratory Study," *Journal of Business Venturing*, Vol. 29, Issue 1, January 2014, pages 1-16.
13. Chance Barnett, "Crowdfunding's Future: Local Online Ecosystems," *Forbes*, posted on March 20, 2013, http://www.forbes.com/sites/chancebarnett/2013/03/20/crowdfundings-future-local-online-ecosystems/, accessed on March 21, 2014.
14. Doug Atkin, interview with Allison Fine, May 7, 2013.
15. Amand Iyer, "How Modern Marketplaces like Uber and Airbnb Build Trust to Achieve Liquidity," TechCrunch, posted on March 4, 2014, http://techcrunch.com/2014/03/04/how-modern-marketplaces-like-uber-and-airbnb-build-trust-to-achieve-liquidity/, accessed on March 18, 2014.
16. Jeremiah Owyang, "The Three Market Drivers: Causes for the Collaborative Economy," Jeremiah Owyang Blog, posted on May 9, 2013, http://www.web-strategist.com/blog/2013/05/09/the-three-market-drivers-causes-for-the-collaborative-economy/, accessed on March 4, 2014.
17. Nancy Scola, "Twitter: An Antidote to Election Day Voting Problems," TechPresident, posted on October 6,

2008, https://techpresident.com/news/5810/twitter-antidote-election-day-voting-problems, accessed on November 15, 2013.
18. Jessica Clark, "Voter Protection, Twitter Style," The American Prospect, November 3, 2008, http://prospect.org/article/voter-protection-twitter-style, accessed on December 11, 2013.
19. Nancy Scola, "Deconstructing (Twitter)Vote Report: Lessons Learned and What's Next," posted on July 8, 2009, https://techpresident.com/news/5810/twitter-antidote-election-day-voting-problems, accessed on December 11, 2013.
20. Jessica Clark, Nina Keim, Public Media 2.0 Field Report: "Building Social Media Infrastructure to Engage Publics: Twitter Vote Report and Inauguration Report '09," American University Center for Social Media, posted in October 2009, http://www.cmsimpact.org/sites/default/files/documents/pages/TVR_Inaug09_Oct.pdf, accessed on December 11, 2013.
21. IRIN, "In-Depth: Kenya's Post Election Crisis," IRIN, Humanitarian News and Analysis, posted on January 7, 2008, http://www.irinnews.org/in-depth/76116/68/kenya-s-post-election-crisis, accessed on December 11, 2013.
22. Simon Jeffery, "Ushahidi: Crowdmapping Collective That Exposed Kenyan Election Killings," *The Guardian* News Blog, posted on April 7, 2011, http://www.theguardian.com/news/blog/2011/apr/07/ushahidi-crowdmap-kenya-violence-hague, accessed on December 12, 2013.
23. Marketing Charts Staff, "Which Forms of Advertising Do Consumers Trust and Act on the Most?", Marketing Charts, posted on September 18, 2013, http://www.marketingcharts.com/wp/television/which-forms-of-

advertising-do-consumers-trust-and-act-on-the-most-36767/, accessed on May 13, 2014.

24. Nicholas Norfolk, "What Is a Brand Ambassador, and How Does a Brand Ambassador Program Work?" Happy Place Marketing, posted on January 24, 2013, http://happyplacemarketing.com/what-is-a-brand-ambassador-and-how-does-a-brand-ambassador, accessed on May 15, 2014.
25. Kevin Briody, Ignite Social Media, "Four Great Examples of Brand Ambassador Programs," posted on March 3, 2010, http://www.ignitesocialmedia.com/lifestyle/brand-ambassador-programs/, accessed on June 15, 2014.
26. Megan Kashner, interview with Allison Fine, February 14, 2014.
27. Megan Kashner, "How Nonprofits Use Crowdfunding to Attract Support of All Kinds," *Chronicle of Philanthropy*, Social Good Podcast, posted on April 17, 2014, http://philanthropy.com/article/How-Nonprofits-Use/145893/, accessed on May 7, 2014.
28. Megan Kashner, "Tapping the Crowd to Solve Social Inequity," Emerging Practitioners in Philanthropy, event podcast, posted on January 22, 2014, http://www.epip.org/2014/01/event-recap-tapping-the-crowd-to-solve-social-inequity/, accessed on February 14, 2014.
29. Amanda Palmer, "The Art of Asking," Ted Talk, posted on February 2013, http://www.ted.com/talks/amanda_palmer_the_art_of_asking, accessed on December 5, 2013.
30. Joshua Clover, "Amanda Palmer's Accidental Experiment with Real Communism," *The New Yorker*, posted on October 2, 2012, http://www.newyorker.com/online/blogs/culture/2012/10/amanda-palmers-

kickstarter-scandal.html, accessed on February 4, 2014.

31. Kronda Adair, interview by email with Allison Fine, February 2, 2014.
32. Peter C. Verhoef, Sander F.M. Beckerse, Jenny van Doorn, "Understand the Perils of Co-Creation," September 2013, *Harvard Business Review*, http://hbr.org/2013/09/understand-the-perils-of-co-creation/ar/1, accessed on November 5, 2013.
33. Francis Gouillart, Douglas Billings, "Community-Powered Problem Solving," *Harvard Business Review*, April 2013, http://hbr.org/2013/04/community-powered-problem-solving/ar/3, accessed on November 11, 2013.
34. John Krause, interview with Allison Fine, February 20, 2014.
35. Daniel Goldstein, interview with Allison Fine, April 23, 2014.
36. Joseph DeSena, interview with Allison Fine, May 18, 2014.
37. Allison Fine, "Healthcare.gov and the Rules of Disengagement," *Stanford Social Innovation Review*, posted on December 18, 2013, http://www.ssireview.org/blog/entry/healthcare.gov_and_the_rules_of_disengagement, accessed on February 6, 2014.
38. Steven Brill, "Obama's Trauma Team, *TIME* Magazine, March 10, 2014, page 3.

Chapter Seven: Creating Cascades of Matterness

1. P. Alex Dow, Lada A. Adamic, Adrien Friggeri, "The Anatomy of Large Facebook Cascades," Association for the Advancement of Artificial Intelligence, 2013, http://friggeri.net/bibliography/papers/Dow2013vf.pdf, page 2, accessed on November 11, 2013.

2. Nicholas A. Christakis and James H. Fowler, *Connected: The Suprising Power of Our Social Networks and How They Shape Our Lives*, Little, Brown and Company, 2009, page 295.
3. Mike Braff, "Stranger Falls Asleep on a Guy's Shoulder on the Subway. Guy Lets Him Sleep," posted on November 1, 2013, http://r2.reddit.com/user/braffination?sort=top, accessed on January 12, 2014.
4. Yasmine Hafitz, "Sleeping Stranger Subway Picture on Q Train Defines Empathy and Is a Lesson in Being Good," Huffington Post Religion, posted on November 6, 2013, http://www.huffingtonpost.com/2013/11/06/sleeping-stranger-subway-picture_n_4228826.html?utm_hp_ref=mostpopular, accessed on January 12, 2013.
5. "Making the Bus Monitor Cry," https://www.youtube.com/watch?feature=player_embedded&v=l93wAqnPQwk#!, posted on June 19, 2012.
6. Seth Stevenson, "Mob Justice," Slate, March 11, 2013, http://www.slate.com/articles/technology/the_browser/2013/03/karen_klein_bullied_bus_monitor_why_did_a_bunch_of_people_on_the_internet.html, accessed on August 13, 2013.
7. Max Siderov, "Let's Give Karen — the bus monitor — H Klein a Vacation!" Indiegogo, campaign started on July 20, 2012, https://www.indiegogo.com/projects/lets-give-karen-the-bus-monitor-h-klein-a-vacation--6, accessed on August 6, 2013.
8. Beth Kanter and Allison Fine, "The Giving Challenge: Assessment and Reflection Report," The Case Foundation, June 22, 2009, http://casefoundation.org/case-studies/giving-challenge-2009, accessed on September 15, 2009.
9. Jack Neff, "Old Spice Is Killing It on YouTube Again, But Sales Are Down Double-Digits," *AdAge*, posted on

August 4, 2011, http://adage.com/article/the-viral-video-chart/spice-killing-youtube-sales/229080/, accessed on August 3, 2013.

10. Tara Hunt, "For Pete's Sake, Brands, Stop Focusing on Viral," LinkedIn, posted on January 9, 2014, https://www.linkedin.com/today/post/article/20140109212537-3154163-for-pete-s-sake-brands-stop-focusing-on-viral?goback=.nmp_*1_*1_*1_*1_*1_*1_*1_*1_*1_*1&trk=object-title, accessed on January 21, 2014.
11. Allison Fine, "A Balanced Look at Text-Message Giving," Social Good Podcast, *Chronicle of Philanthropy,* posted on February 10, 2010, http://philanthropy.com/article/A-Balanced-Look-at/64102/, accessed on October 5, 2013.
12. Ed Keller, "Word-of-Mouth Goes Mainstream, Is Now Measurable," *AdAge,* posted on February 6, 2013, http://adage.com/article/guest-columnists/word-mouth-mainstream-measurable/239501/, accessed on May 15, 2014.
13. Yu-Hao Lee, Gary Hsieh, "Does Slactivism Hurt Activism? The Effects of Moral Balancing and Consistency in Online Activism," Proceedings of the SIGCHI Conference on Human Factors in Computing Systems, April 27-May 2, 2013, page 811-820, http://dl.acm.org/citation.cfm?id=2470770, accessed October 4, 2013.
14. Allison Fine, "Lessons From the It Gets Better Project," Social Good podcast, *Chronicle of Philanthropy,* posted on November 8, 2010, http://philanthropy.com/article/Lessons-From-the-It-Gets/125250/, accessed on October 21, 2013.
15. It Gets Better, http://www.itgetsbetter.org/pages/about-it-gets-better-project/, accessed on March 20, 2014.

16. 92nd Street Y, "Giving Tuesday FAQs," https://community.givingtuesday.org/page/faq, accessed on January 12, 2014.
17. Jeanne Allen, "Giving Tuesday 2013: More Infrastructure, More Money, More Groups in the Mix," *Nonprofit Quarterly*, posted on December 6, 2013, https://nonprofitquarterly.org/policysocial-context/23349-giving-tuesday-2013-more-infrastructure-more-money-more-groups-in-the-mix.html, accessed on March 2, 2014.
18. Robert M. Bond, Christopher J. Farris, Jason J. Jones, Adam D. I. Kramer, Cameron Marlow, Jaime E. Settle, James Fowler, "A 61-Million-Person Experiment in Social Influence and Political Mobilization," *Nature*, Vol 489, September 13, 2012, page 295-298.
19. Monica Gaudio, "A Tale of Two Tarts," Gode Cookery Presents, posted in 2005 (exact date unclear) http://www.godecookery.com/twotarts/twotarts.html, accessed on November 13, 2013.
20. Monica Gaudio, "Copyright Infringement and Me," posted on November 3, 2010, http://illadore.livejournal.com/30674.html, accessed on November 13, 2013.
21. Nick Mamatas, "Copyright Follies," November 3, 2010, http://nihilistic-kid.livejournal.com/1553538.html, accessed on November 13, 2013.
22. Linda Holmes, "The Day the Internet Threw a Righteous Hissyfit About Copyright and Pie," posted on November 5, 2010, http://www.npr.org/blogs/monkeysee/2010/11/05/131091599/the-day-the-internet-threw-a-righteous-hissyfit-about-copyright-and-pie, accessed on November 13, 2013.
23. Ron Doyle, "Are *Cooks Source* Magazine and Judith Griggs Innocent?" posted on November 8, 2010, *Psychology Today*, http://www.psychologytoday.com/blog/you-20/201011/are-cooks-source-

magazine-and-judith-griggs-innocent, accessed on November 13, 2013.

24. Comment posted by senshikittie on November 4, 2010, http://illadore.livejournal.com/30674.html?page=2, accessed on November 13, 2013.
25. Lisa Khoury, "Why Put a Bumper Sticker on a Ferrari?" *The Spectrum*, The Independent Student Publication of the University at Buffalo, published on January 28, 2012, http://www.ubspectrum.com/mobile/opinion/why-put-a-bumper-sticker-on-a-ferrari-1.27557890, accessed on October 20, 2013. [Note: the original post appears to be removed from the Spectrum site; it can be accessed at https://www.youtube.com/watch?v=FusKUU82YY0]
26. Rebecca Bratek, Sara Dinatale, "Tatoo Column Goes Viral," *The Spectrum*, The Independent Student Publication of the University at Buffalo, posted on February 2, 2012, http://www.ubspectrum.com/news/view.php/278087/Tattoo-Column-Goes-Viral#.UoYqeI2hAZ5, accessed on October 20, 2013.
27. Lisa Khoury, "The Day I Met the Internet," *The Spectrum*, The Independent Student Publication of the University at Buffalo, posted on February 2, 2012, http://www.ubspectrum.com/news/view.php/277166/The-Day-I-Met-the-Internet, accessed on October 20, 2013.
28. Dan Reimold, "6 Ways to Survive an Internet Drubbing," PBS Media Shift, posted on June 5, 2013, http://www.pbs.org/mediashift/2013/06/how-to-avoid-survive-fight-back-against-an-internet-drubbing/, accessed on November 20, 2013.
29. Lisa Khoury, interview with Allison Fine, November 21, 2013.
30. Adrien Chen, "Unmasking Reddit's Violentacrez, The Biggest Troll on the Web," Gawker, posted on October

12, 2012, http://gawker.com/5950981/unmasking-reddits-violentacrez-the-biggest-troll-on-the-web, accessed on November 5, 2013.

31. Fernando Alfonso, III, "Reddit's Most Notorious Troll Loses Job After Gawker Profile," The Daily Dot, Posted on October 15, 2012, http://www.dailydot.com/news/violentacrez-reddit-troll-fired-gawker-profile/, accessed on November 5, 2013.
32. Philbert de Zwart, commenting on "6 Ways to Survive an Internet Drubbing," PBS Media Shift, posted on June 5, 2013, http://www.pbs.org/mediashift/2013/06/how-to-avoid-survive-fight-back-against-an-internet-drubbing/, accessed on November 20, 2013.

Chapter Eight: A Call for Collective Responsibility

1. Peter Levine, *We Are the Ones We've Been Waiting For: The Promise of Civic Renewal in America*, Oxford University Press, 2013, page 18.
2. Penn Live Editorial Board, "Unopposed Races: Too Many Pennsylvania Legislators Run for Re-Election With No Competition," November 15, 2012, http://www.pennlive.com/opinion/index.ssf/2012/11/unopposed_races_too_many_pennsylvania_legislators_run_unopposed.html, accessed on July 15, 2014.
3. Jake Brewer, interview with Allison Fine, July 2, 2014.
4. Noel Hidalgo, interview with Allison Fine, July 23, 2013.
5. Nancy Tate, interview with Allison Fine, October 28, 2011.
6. Susan Page, Poll: Public Service Valued; Politics Not-So-Much, USA Today, posted on July 22, 2013,

http://www.usatoday.com/story/news/nation/2013/07/21/public-service-valued-politics--not-so-much/2573743/, accessed on August 12, 2014.

7. Levine, *op. cit.*, page 12.
8. Rebecca MacKinnon, *Consent of the Networked,* page 17.
9. Jaron Lanier, *You Are Not a Gadget*, Vintage Books, 2010, page 82.
10. Blantham, comment on, "Community-Powered Problem Solving," HBR.org, http://hbr.org/2013/04/community-powered-problem-solving/ar/3, accessed on February 12, 2014.

43966117R00146

Made in the USA
Middletown, DE
24 May 2017